I0624048

Proceeds from the book will be donated
to the First Lady Scholarship
at South Carolina State University.

Mr. President, I've Got Your Back!

The First Ladies of
South Carolina State University

Mr. President, I've Got Your Back!

The First Ladies of South Carolina State University

Abbiegail H. Hugine
Mary L. Smalls

Fresh Ink Group
Guntersville

Mr. President, I've Got Your Back!

The First Ladies of
South Carolina State University

Copyright © 2024
by Abbiegail Mariam Hamilton Hugine
Mary L. Smalls

Fresh Ink Group
An Imprint of:
The Fresh Ink Group, LLC
1021 Blount Avenue #931
Guntersville, AL 35976
Email: info@FreshInkGroup.com
FreshInkGroup.com

Edition 1.0 2024

Cover design by Stephen Geez / FIG
Book design by Amit Dey / FIG
Associate publisher Beem Weeks / FIG

Cataloging-in-Publication Recommendations:
HIS056000 HISTORY / African American & Black
EDU016000 EDUCATION / History
HIS036120 HISTORY / United States / State & Local / South

Library of Congress Control Number: 2024904251

ISBN-13: 978-1-958922-89-7 Softcover
ISBN-13: 978-1-958922-90-3 Hardcover
ISBN-13: 978-1-958922-91-0 Ebooks

Mr. President, I've Got Your Back!
The First Ladies of
South Carolina State University

TABLE OF CONTENTS

FOREWORD

Throughout our storied history, the presidents of what is now South Carolina State University have shepherded the institution from its humble beginnings as an Agricultural, Mechanical, and Normal school to the complex university we know today. As the thirteenth president of SC State, I have inherited the fruits of their hard work and dedication to the cause.

Many of the former presidents of SC State University had a lot of help and support from their spouses, who were affectionately known as the "First Ladies" of the institution. Despite their immense contributions, their hard work and dedication often went unnoticed and unappreciated. However, their role was just as significant as their husbands, and they played a crucial part in their success. Each First Lady made a valuable contribution to the success of her husband's presidency.

Each First Lady contributed to the institution's successes in her unique fashion. Often, they sacrificed their aspirations to support their husbands, their families, and the students of SC State. The vast accomplishments of our presidents have been well documented in the annals of SC State's history, but for too long, the contributions of their partners in life have gone unrecognized.

There is no one better suited to correct this mistake than Mrs. Abbiegail H. Hugine. She is a highly accomplished educator and represents the true essence of the title 'First Lady' at the institution. Ms. Mary L. Smalls, a retired librarian and archival resource at SC State, provided valuable assistance in this endeavor. She has worked with many first ladies on various initiatives.

To say the least, this book is long overdue.

I speak from a place of love and admiration because my dear partner, Agatha Youmans Conyers, has been my anchor throughout my adult life. She brings her unique talents and ideas to SC State, and for that, I am forever grateful.

Agatha and I are passionate about serving the students of South Carolina State University. One of my aims is to establish a permanent method of recognizing the significant contributions of our First Ladies on campus. It's crucial to honor their legacy and ensure that their contributions are not forgotten. Mrs. Hugine has set a remarkable example with her comprehensive and engaging book.

We are deeply indebted to Mrs. Hugine and Ms. Smalls for their detailed research and care in producing this essential gift to SC State's historical records.

Colonel (Retired) Alexander Conyers
Thirteenth President
South Carolina State University

PREFACE

A Writer's Perspective
By Abbiegail H. Hugine

Of the millions of people in the United States, there are the fortunate few who have the opportunity to serve as the President of the United States. Since the founding of the country, forty-six persons (46) have held the position of president. The first ladies of the United States serve in roles with their spouses. There are presidents of colleges and universities. Their spouses also serve with them.

Some individuals view the role of a First Lady as a ceremonial role. However, the president's spouse plays a significant role as an ambassador for the university, a listening ear for the president, an able advisor, and a person who keeps her ear to the ground. The president's spouse is the person who provides an honest assessment of issues without having an ulterior motive. Serving as First Lady carries a lot of responsibilities for faculty, students, staff, programs, and other operations to be successful. Regrettably, success may or may not be accomplished for various reasons including political upheavals, scandals, illnesses, lack of resources, and the list continues. Finally, the success the president achieves is, to a great extent, dependent upon the supportive "First Lady." In the present day, it could be a "First Gentleman" or significant other.

At South Carolina State University (SCSU), there have been twelve (12) First Ladies. I served as the First Lady when my husband, Dr. Andrew Hugine, Jr., was named the ninth President from 2003-2007.

First ladies are indeed the unsung heroes. While it is impossible to adequately delineate and discuss all of their contributions in this book, we will give a glimpse of the role of the First Ladies and how their experiences on campus may have affected them. The book will chronicle the lives of the phenomenal and impactful First Ladies of South Carolina State University from 1896-2023.

THE FIRST LADIES

First Lady Anna Marie Hume Miller, 1896–1911

First Lady Miller was married to Dr. Thomas Ezekiel Miller, who was the First President of The Colored Normal, Industrial, Agricultural, and Mechanical College of Orangeburg, South Carolina. She was a loving and devoted wife, and a mother to nine children, of whom seven survived to adulthood. Dr. Miller was both an educator and a lawyer, and their family was deeply involved in the fields of politics and education, which gave them a solid foundation.

Establishing the college was a complex process, and Mrs. Miller played a vital role in supporting her husband in various operational tasks, including identifying facilities, planning programs, hiring faculty, and recruiting students. Both President and First Lady Miller worked tirelessly to create a friendly, affordable, comfortable, and welcoming environment that enabled students to enhance their experience at the college.

First Lady Marion Raven Birnie Wilkinson, 1911–1932

From the early record, First Lady Wilkinson had a similar task to First Lady Miller in that the college was still in its infancy. In her role as First Lady, she was a leading humanitarian in South Carolina committed to improving the lives of the less fortunate in the community of Orangeburg and surrounding areas.

At the college, she joined her husband, President Robert Shaw Wilkinson, the Second President, in celebrating the 25th Anniversary of the school and the growth and development that took place during the college's first quarter of a century of existence.

First Lady Julia Elizabeth Allen Turner, 1950–1967

Mrs. Turner became the First Lady after the college had gone without one for over eighteen years. She was married to Dr. Benner C. Turner, the Fourth President.

During the Turner administration, major developments occurred at the college. The General Assembly changed the school's name to South Carolina State College, and it became a member of the Southern Association of Colleges and Schools (SACS), which granted it full accreditation. The Association of American Colleges also accredited the institution. The college experienced growth, with increases in enrollment, degree programs, facilities, and doctoral faculty. Throughout these years of change, First Lady Turner provided valuable support to her husband.

First Lady Julie Etta Washington Nance, 1968–1986

Julie was born on the campus of South Carolina State College. Forty-two years later, she became First Lady in 1968. She brought an aura of grace, charm, and engagement to the position. First Lady Nance and her husband, President M. Maceo Nance, Jr., the Fifth President, were the consummate official university host and hostess. Both were people-friendly and frequently entertained faculty, staff, and others in their home. First Lady Nance was an ambassador extraordinaire for the college and the students. In her role, she nurtured the students and provided leadership to faculty and staff. I had the honor to be in her presence, and most of what I learned about being a First Lady came from Mrs. Nance.

Julie devoted her entire life to the university and the community. She experienced many good days on campus. She also experienced campus tragedy when three students were killed in the Orangeburg Massacre on February 8, 1968. Andrew and I were freshmen on campus during this tragic time.

First Lady Sadie Burris Smith, 1986–1992

In 1986, President Albert Emanuel Smith, the Sixth President, and First Lady Sadie Burris Smith joined the South Carolina State College family. The Smiths worked to secure partnerships with major corporations. First Lady Smith's community involvement was the Children's Reading Program at the Orangeburg County Library. She was a staunch supporter of Felton Laboratory School.

Mrs. Smith inaugurated the First Lady's Luncheon for campus and community women. Since 1987, every First Lady has held the event annually.

A highlight of her role as First Lady was serving as a university hostess when Mrs. Barbara Bush, First Lady of the United States and wife of President George W. Bush, was conferred an honorary doctorate.

First Lady Parthelia Davis Carpenter, 1992

After President Smith left the university, Dr. Carl A. Carpenter was named Interim President. During his tenure, there were efforts to increase enrollment, a Master of Arts degree in teaching was initiated, the fine arts building was approved, and the college was designated a university. Always a supportive wife, First Lady Carpenter ably assisted Interim President Carpenter during this period. Being a parent, she exhibited a particularly fond affinity for the students.

First Lady Christine McGill Davis, 1996–2002

During a significant time in the university's history, First Lady Davis played an important role as the official university hostess alongside her husband, President Leroy Davis, the Eighth President. They presided over the centennial celebration, which involved a plethora of activities and functions, keeping her busy as First Lady. Her wit and charm were always welcoming to everyone she met, and she had a great fondness for the students.

Other milestones during this period were the accreditation of the School of Business by the Association to Advance Collegiate Schools of Business (AACSB) and the reaffirmation of accreditation by the Southern Association of Colleges and Schools (SACS). She continued the First Lady's Scholarship Luncheon, and the university held its first annual scholarship gala.

First Lady Frances Davenport Finney, 2002–2003

On July 1, 2002, the Board named retired Chief Justice of the South Carolina Supreme Court, Ernest A. Finney, Jr., as Interim President. First Lady Finney, with an outgoing and vivacious personality, had no problems interacting and engaging the faculty, staff, and students.

Affectionally called "Ladybug," her prints were left on campus through several initiatives, including building a gazebo in the center of the campus, which remains there today, and organizing the Bulldog Round-Up Committee which dedicated their efforts to beautifying the campus.

First Lady Abbiegail Mariam Hamilton Hugine, 2003–2007

When her husband, Dr. Andrew Hugine, Jr. was named the Ninth President, First Lady Abbiegail Hugine had a dilemma. Should she become a full-time First Lady or continue her role as an administrator? Eventually, as an administrator, her love for teaching and impacting the lives of young people was selected. Moreover, she did an exceptional job of balancing the two roles. Her school received multiple honors, and she ably carried out the many duties of the First Lady.

First Lady Hugine hosted social events on campus, four First Lady Scholarship Luncheons, and often engaged with students. She assisted in fostering the university by joining and supporting her husband on many recruitment events and traveling to meet alumni.

A highlight of her tenure was serving as hostess for the First Democratic National Debate of the 2007 Campaign for the United States President. South Carolina State University was the first HBCU to have the distinction of hosting the debate. The national exposure for the university was immeasurable. The debaters included Senator Barack Obama, who became president; Senator Joe Biden who also became president, and Senator Hillary Clinton, who served as Secretary of State under President Obama.

First Lady Diane Shaw Cooper, 2008–2012

First Lady Diane accompanied her husband, President George E. Cooper, the Tenth President to South Carolina State University from the Maryland/DC area after both had stellar careers in education. For First Lady Cooper, it was returning home to Kingstree, South Carolina where she was born.

The Cooper years saw an expansion into international education and partnerships. The partnership with Tanzania provided a platform for First Lady Cooper to host international dignitaries. They shared an interest in student development and recruitment and worked with the students to bring these interests to fruition.

Diane was also successful in bringing noted celebrities to the campus. For the 2010 First Lady's Luncheon, Donna Brazile, a renowned television political commentator and analyst, was the keynote speaker. While she enjoyed this aspect of her role, in an interview with Dionne Gleaton at *The Times and Democrat*, First Lady Diane said that her greatest joy was the students at South Carolina State University. She also assisted with a mentoring program for twenty young ladies at Felton Laboratory School called the "First Ladies Little Ladies Club."

First Lady Monedia K. Elzey, 2013–2015

First Lady Elzey accompanied her husband, Mr. Thomas J. Elzey, the Eleventh President, to South Carolina State University from The Citadel in Charleston, South Carolina. She was the only First Lady with an earned Ph.D.

First Lady Elzey continued the tradition of hosting the First Lady's Scholarship Luncheon, which aimed to raise funds for students and promote women's advancement. As part of the event held on February 28, 2014, she invited Carol Moseley-Braun, the first African American woman to be elected to the United States Senate, to be the keynote speaker.

First Lady Elsey actively engaged with students on campus and sought ways to enhance their career prospects. She established a First Lady's Clothing Boutique to provide students with professional attire for job interviews.

First Lady Agatha Youmans Conyers, 2021–

When Colonel (Retired) Alexander Conyers was named the Thirteenth President in 2021, he became the fifth graduate of the university to hold the office, following in the footsteps of Nance, Carpenter, Davis, and Hugine. Likewise, First Lady Agatha Youmans Conyers became the fifth First Lady graduate of the university, following in the footsteps of First Ladies Nance, Carpenter, Davis, and Hugine.

President and First Lady Conyers are often dubbed the power couple. Since his appointment, the university has seen an increase in enrollment and funding at all levels: federal, state, local, and alumni.

With a certificate in philanthropy, First Lady Conyers took an active role in assisting her husband and the university in a goal to raise $1.25 million for the 125th Anniversary of the university and to honor the years of education and service. First Lady Agatha initiated a South Carolina State University (SCSU) Legacy Program to encourage graduates to send their children to the university and recognize students for continuing the Bulldog tradition of excellence.

First Lady Conyers dedicated her First Lady's Scholarship Luncheon to a scholarship fund for all university students.

The influences of these First Ladies have had a major impact on the development, progress, and legacy of SCSU. As one of these dynamic First Ladies, I was honored to have been a part of the rich history of SCSU.

Some women had the early vision to recognize the potential of leadership in their life partners. They, with their fresh attitudes, pushed, pulled or walked beside their mates until dreams became realities. This rare breed of women is known as . . .

First Ladies

First Ladies must be vigilant in their thinking from the start

To derive pride from their performance and goodness within their heart

To visualize the end product, they must have a strong will

And be aware that success is not a one-step deal

They know that confidence builds slowly with daily reinforcement

And every request must be scrutinized before giving their consent

Their position as a First Lady is a profession in itself

And from the outside looking in, may represent some wealth

Their partners (College Presidents) compete against people of all kind

So to enrich and support their mates, they must devote their energy and time

Encouraging their interest

Pushing them gently to explore their talents

Praising them frequently

And loving them unconditionally

For benefits are numerous when they think logically and are kind

And surround themselves among those with wisdom which is sound

They must be patiently disciplined and as structured as they can

Don't spend without a budget; don't live without a plan

They must train themselves to think positively which is really an attitude

That embraces the wealth of the human experience, using the mind as a tool

To turn negatives into positives with a stream of progressive thoughts

That abundance is unlimited if they don't dwell on lack or faults

First Ladies must have a heavy dose of self-love to survive

To make themselves comfortable, forgiving and accepting of others and their lives

They may not get much praise so they must quickly learn

To celebrate themselves and still make time for fun

For each of them brings to the table their unique and individual style

They can't please everyone but they can always wear a smile

Whether advising students; entertaining guests

Hosting a dinner or giving an address

Coordinating a program; sing a song

Planting a garden or correcting a wrong

Spearheading a committee; a partner to their spouse

Welcoming dignitaries; keeping an open mind and house

These are just a few of the duties they graciously perform

With blessings from the Great Spirit above

They put their faith in action, with fortitude to win,

We salute them one and all, pledging our love!

Barbara Randall Clark
Orangeburg, South Carolina
February 27, 2004

Photo: *Miller with his wife, ca. 1924. Wikipedia*

FIRST LADY
ANNA MARIE HUME MILLER

The Colored Normal, Industrial, Agricultural and Mechanical College, 1896 - 1911

One hundred twenty-eight years ago, The Colored Normal, Industrial, Agricultural and Mechanical College welcomed her first, **First Lady, Mrs. Anna Marie Hume Miller**. Mrs. Miller, the wife of Dr. Thomas Ezekiel Miller, the First President, served as First Lady from 1896 – 1911.

Anna Marie Hume was born in Charleston, South Carolina to parents William Hume and Julia Robinson on September 20, 1853. She had two younger brothers, William Hume (1857-1920) and Edward P. Hume (1860-1924).

Mr. Thomas Ezekiel Miller was well trained in and educated in politics and education before his marriage to Anna Marie Hume in 1874 in Charleston. The Millers had nine children, seven of whom survived childhood: John Hume Miller (1876-1953); Mary J. Miller Earle (1879-1958); Thomas Ezekiel Miller, Jr. (1880-1954); Pansy E. Miller Maxwell (1885-1976); Victor George Miller (1888-1890); Marie Miller (1890-1890); Marguerite E. Edwards; Anna Miller Cooke; and Harry C. Miller (1893-1955). The children grew up in a political and educational environment during the Jim Crow era of racial segregation in the South.

According to the 1880 Census, Anna Miller, who was 26 years old at the time, was listed as the housekeeper in the household of Thomas Miller, who was 30 years old, at Coosawhatchie, Beaufort, South Carolina. On the other hand, the 1910 Census shows that Anna M. Miller, who was 52 years old, worked as a dressmaker and was listed as the wife of Thomas E. Miller, who was 60 years old, in Ward 5, Orangeburg, South Carolina. Both dates are recorded in wikitree-1448.

During her time as First Lady, Mrs. Miller and President Miller worked to enhance student life at the college. They provided dining area furnishings, proper kitchen utensils, and meals to students for $5.00 per month.

After leaving the position as First Lady in 1911, the Millers returned to Charleston. In 1921 they moved to Powelton Village in Philadelphia, a neighborhood with few blacks at that time. They returned to Charleston in the early 1930s.

Miller House: Thomas E. Miller and his wife, Anna, resided in this house at 3405 Hamilton Street in *Powelton which they purchased in 1921 and shared with their daughter Pansy and her husband, Dr. Charles W. Maxwell. West Philadelphia Collaborative History*

Mrs. Miller died on September 26, 1936, at 83 years old. *The Pittsburg Courier* reported that her survivors were her husband, President Miller, and six children who attended the funeral: Mrs. Pansy E. Miller Maxwell and Mrs. Margaret Miller Edwards, Atlantic City, New Jersey; Mrs. Anna Miller Cooke, Minnesota; Dr. John Hume Miller, Chester, Pennsylvania; and Dr. Thomas E. Miller, Jr. and Mr. Harry H. Miller of Charleston. The Miller's tombstone in the Brotherly Association Cemetery in Charleston reads *ANNA M. HUME, MY VIRTUOUS, LOYAL, DEVOUT WIFE, A CHRISTIAN, SELF-SACRIFICING, LOVEABLE MOTHER. Dr. Miller died in Charleston on April 8, 1938, and is buried next to Anna in the* Brotherly Association Cemetery.

Photo *Find a Grave*

BIBLIOGRAPHY

- "Anna M. (Hume) Miller (1853-1936)." WikiTree, December 1, 2022. https://www.wikitree.com/wiki/Hume-1448

- "Anna Marie Hume Miller." Find a Grave, Anonymous, June 9, 2004. https://www.findagrave.com/memorial/8894090/anna-marie-miller

- Ewbank, Douglas. "Thomas E. Miller: A Life in Service to Civil Rights." Philadelphia, PA, West Philadelphia Collaborative History. https://collaborativehistory.gse.upenn.edu/stories/thomas-e-miller

- "Ex-Congressman Miller's Wife Dies In S.C." *The Pittsburg Courier*, October 10, 1936, p. 5.

- "Powelton History Blog: A Collective Biography of a Philadelphia Neighborhood." Blogspot, February 2, 2013. https://poweltonhistoryblog.blogspot.com/2013/02/

- South Carolina State University Historical Collection. First Lady Scholarship Luncheon program, *"Embracing Our Legacy and Building Our Future Through Excellence."* February 27, 2004, p. 4.

- "Thomas E. Miller." Wikipedia, March 17, 2023. https://en.wikipedia.org/wiki/Thomas_E._Miller

Photo: *Sunlight Club Website*

FIRST LADY
MARION RAVEN BIRNIE WILKINSON

The Colored Normal, Industrial,
Agricultural and Mechanical College, 1911 – 1932

Mrs. Marion Raven Birnie Wilkinson was born on June 23, 1870 in Charleston, South Carolina to Richard Birnie and Anna Frost. She was the eldest daughter of four siblings, Charles Wainwright Birnie (1874-1938); Hildegarde Birnie Beard (1878-1945); Anna Laurance Birnie (1878-1918); and Richard Birnie, Jr. (1881-1968). *The South Carolina Encyclopedia* described the Birnies and the family of Anna Frost as descendants of antebellum-free black families and members of Charleston's black elite. Her father and her uncle, Charles Wainwright Birnie, were wealthy cotton shipping agents.

Marion's family valued education and service, and she also embraced these principles throughout her life. She received her early education at the well-respected Avery Institute in Charleston, South Carolina. Marion graduated with honors in 1888 and went on to teach at the Institute for nine years. Her studies at Avery helped her develop a strong sense of community service, which greatly influenced her career in social and political change.

Mrs. Wilkinson celebrates her 85th birthday. She is pictured with her children Dr. Robert S. Wilkinson, Mrs. Helen Sheffield, Dr. Frost B. Wilkinson, and Miss Lula Wilkinson Bulldog Yearbook, 1957

On June 29, 1897, Marion Raven Birnie married Robert Shaw Wilkinson. They were the parents of four accomplished children, Helen Raven Wilkinson Sheffield (1898-1970), Dr. Robert Shaw Wilkinson, Jr. (1899-1984); Frost Birnie Wilkinson, DDS (1902-1995); and Lula Love Wilkinson (1905-1994).

Mrs. Wilkinson, the wife of Dr. Robert Shaw Wilkinson who was the second President of the institution, served as the First Lady from 1911 to 1932. During her tenure, she actively participated in campus activities and took charge of various responsibilities. She supervised the women's dormitory, managed the dining hall, worked with the Domestic Science Department, welcomed guests, and acted as a mentor to students. Her love and respect for the students made her known as "Mother Wilkinson." Additionally, she loved flowers, and her keen interest played a significant role in enhancing the beauty of the campus.

Together, the Wilkinsons worked to feed the spiritual needs of the students. The inscription on the St. Paul's Episcopal Church markers by Devry Becker Jones, editor, and Dave W, photographer reads:

"In 1912, First Lady Wilkinson and President Wilkinson founded St. Paul's Episcopal Church in Orangeburg as St. Paul's Episcopal Mission. Worship

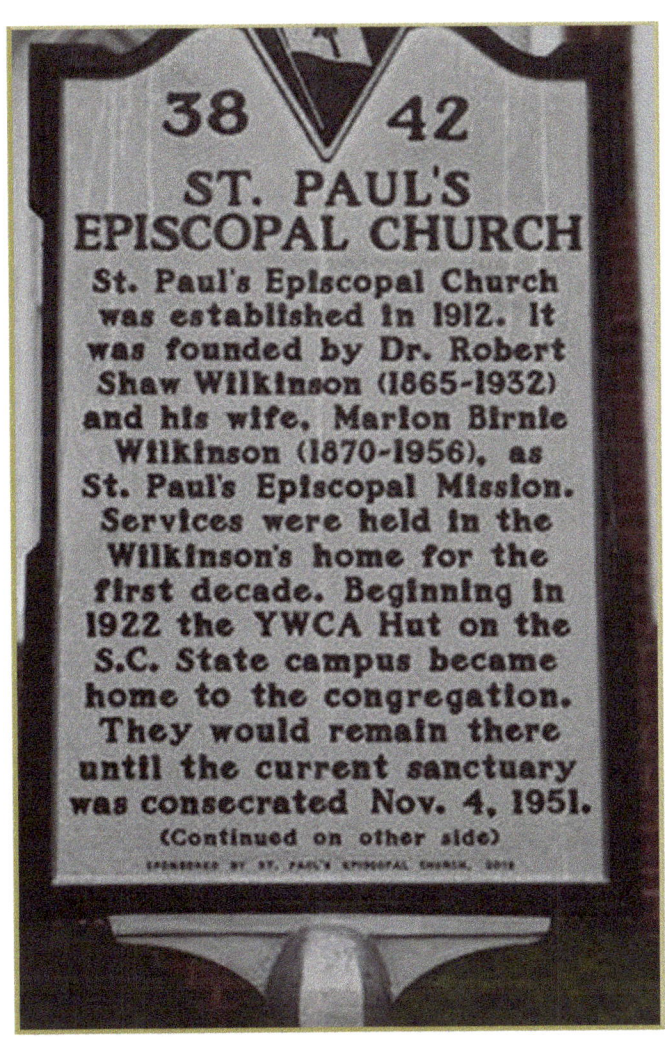

Side 1: Photographed by: Dave W, May 17, 2023

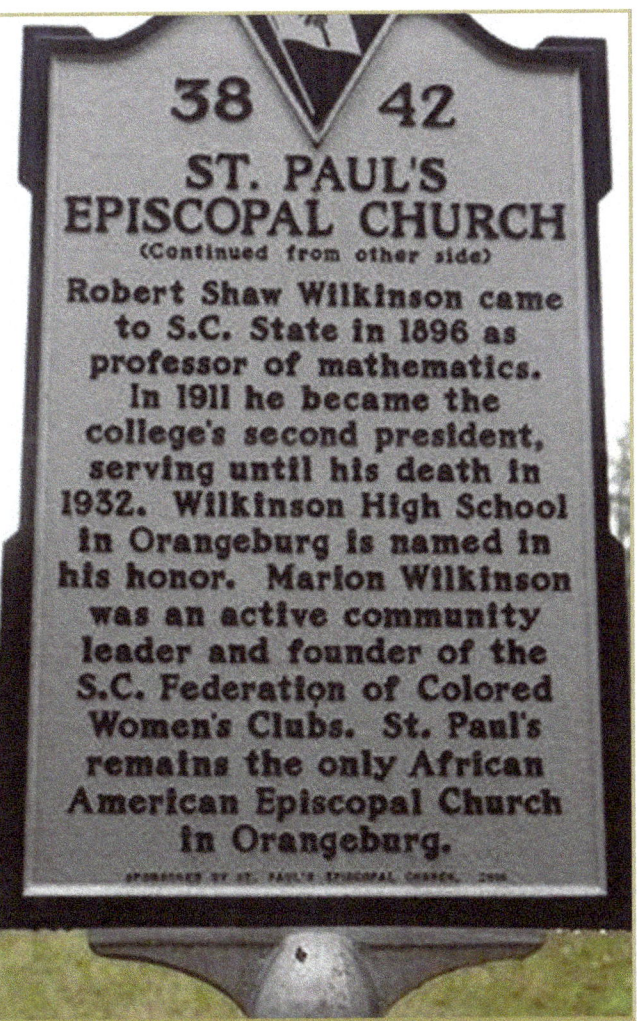

Side 2: Photographed by: Dave W, May 17, 2023

services were held in the Wilkinson's home for the first decade. Beginning in 1922, the YWCA (Young Women Christian Association) Hut located on the campus of The Colored Normal, Industrial, Agricultural, and Mechanical College became home to the congregation. They remained there until the current sanctuary was consecrated on November 4, 1951."

First Lady Wilkinson served as the main advisor to the YMCA. By 1928, her leadership resulted in the construction of the only YWCA building on a historically African American college campus.

"From an early age, Wilkinson was interested in social reform efforts in South Carolina and encouraged educated, middle-class African American women to

MARION BIRNIE WILKINSON HOME FOR GIRLS

South Carolina Federation of Women's and Youth Clubs, Inc.

share their knowledge and material resources with those less fortunate," as stated in *The South Carolina Encyclopedia.*

According to *Wikipedia*, "The South Carolina Federation of Colored Women's Clubs (SCFCWC) "was an African American women's club founded in 1909 in South Carolina. The umbrella organization was created by Marion Bernie Wilkinson, Sara B. Henderson, Lizella A. Jenkins Moorer, Celia Dial Saxon and other women who met at Sydney Park Church in Columbia. hey adopted the motto of the National Association of Colored Women's Clubs (NACWC), "Lifting as We Climb." Wilkinson became the first president of SCFCWC and worked towards improving education and living conditions for black people in South Carolina. The organization grew to have twenty-five hundred members in 1922. One of the major accomplishments of the SCFCWC was the creation of the Wilkinson Home for Colored Girls in Cayce. The home was originally for girls who had been deemed "delinquent" and later housed orphans. SCFCWC also raised money for other organizations and causes and ran food drives. In 1960, the organization became a United Way agency."

"From the beginning, the SCFCWC aimed to improve education, hold an educational convention annually, protect women and children in the home and at work, further political security and rights, and promote interracial understanding. Black women at the time understood the importance of forming ties with white women in their fight for equality. The white women active in SCFCWC often were committed to improving African American lives, but they still upheld racial norms."

Not only was First Lady Wilkinson a trustee of the Marion Birnie Wilkinson Home for Underprivileged Orphans in Cayce, South Carolina, but other Clubs bearing her name included the Marion Birnie Wilkinson Federation Club in Chester, South Carolina, and the Marion Birnie Wilkinson Club in Charleston.

The South Carolina Federation of Colored Women's Clubs held its eighth annual session in Orangeburg. The members have put up 20,790 cans of fruits and vegetables and have contributed $8,000 to the Red Cross, the Y. M. C. A. and camp activities.

Cayton's Weekly, a newspaper out of Seattle, Washington, highlights the efforts and activities of the SCFCWC in their September 21, 1918 issue. *South Carolina Digital Newspaper Program*

1959 Executive Board of the South Carolina Federation of Colored Women's Clubs in session in front of the Wilkinson Home. *South Carolina Federation of Women's and Youth Clubs, Inc.*

In the 1940s, black women in South Carolina utilized the SCFCWC to advocate for equal pay for teachers, voting rights, full citizenship, and support for middle-class black women. The SCFCWC also worked to ensure African Americans were included in the political process. *Wikipedia*

In the April 1940 issues of *The Southern Frontier*, it states, "Today the Wilkinson Home is owned and operated by Negro women of South Carolina. They have received no state or federal aid. The Duke Foundation makes a small contribution of $600 but the bulk of the money—last year it amounted to $3,587.66—is raised through the efforts of Negro women of the State Federation of Colored Women."

"There are thirty-five children in the home, ages five to fourteen. They attend either the local school or the Booker Washington High School of Columbia. In addition, in the home itself, they are taught sewing, handicraft, cooking, housecleaning laundering, poultry raising and dairying under the supervision of Mrs. Mamie Felder, the home mother. They attend church and Sunday school nearby."

The Sisterhood: SC Suffragists' series gave recognition to Mrs. Wilkinson's influence on the women's right movement. In *Knowitall it is stated,*

"As the national debate for suffrage came to the fore, South Carolina women were increasingly drawn into the movement for social and educational reform. From the Women's Christian Temperance Union (WCTU) to the Equal Suffrage Leagues (ESL) to the burgeoning women's club movement, numerous groups - both Black and White -mobilized and took valiant stands as the fight for suffrage intensified. Susan Pringle Frost, Eulalie Salley, **Marion Birnie Wilkinson** *and the Pollitzer Sisters - Mabel, Carrie, and Anita, daughters of a prominent Jewish family from Charleston - are among the oft-overlooked and forgotten rebels in the Palmetto State. Their tireless efforts contributed greatly to the women's rights movement and the fight for the female vote."*

Before Restoration: The Great Branch Rosenwald Teacherage

After Restoration: *The Great Branch Rosenwald Teacherage*

First Lady Wilkinson organized the first Rosenwald School in South Carolina. It was located in the Great Branch Community on the Neeses Highway in Orangeburg to enhance educational facilities for African Americans.

The Great Branch School was built in 1922 - 1923 at a cost of $2550. The teacher's home, one of only eight built in South Carolina in 1924-1925 at a cost of $2650. Today, only two of the eight are still standing. One is on the campus of South Carolina State University, and the other is in Great Branch. The home was built to house the principal and teachers who were employed by the school but lived too far from school to commute on a daily basis. We have records showing that at least three principals lived in the home. In 2007, the house was listed on the National Register of Historical Place. Great Branch Rosenwald Teacherage

In 1910, First Lady Wilkinson founded and became the president of the Sunlight Club, the first African American women's organization in Orangeburg. It was dedicated to performing charitable acts for fellow citizens.

First Lady Wilkinson's contributions impacted many on more than a state-wide level. She was an advisor to the Hoover administration on child welfare programs; helped to establish a training school and nursery as part of the Works Progress Administration (WPA); chaired the South Carolina State College YWCA Advisory Board; led the state Commission on Interracial Cooperation; was an officer in the International Council of Women of the Darker Races; a member of the County Executive Committee of the Red Cross; and was a member of the Board of Trustees of Voorhees College, Denmark, South Carolina. During World War I, First Lady Wilkinson and other African American club women organized recreation centers for African American soldiers. The National Association of Colored Women's Clubs (NACWC) was founded in 1896 and spearheaded the black women's club movement. Mrs. Wilkinson was its third president.

Added By Juanda Owens B. *Find a Grave*

During her time, Benjamin Mays, President of Morehouse College, described Mrs. Wilkinson as "South Carolina's outstanding Negro woman; indeed, in programs designed to help the poor and improve race relations, in my opinion, she was the leading woman in South Carolina."

She died in Orangeburg on September 19, 1956, and was laid to rest in the Orangeburg Cemetery with President Wilkinson who passed on March 13, 1932.

Photo: *Marion B. Wilkinson. Wikipedia*

Photo: Dr. Robert S. Wilkinson, circa 1920
Celebrating the Collections of Historically Black Colleges and Universities

BIBLIOGRAPHY

- "About Us – The Sunlight Club." https://sunlightclub.org/about-us
- boydkf. "From Socialization to Social Change: Women's Clubs of South Carolina." South Carolina Digital Newspaper Program, March 27, 2013. https://digital.library.sc.edu/blogs/newspaper/2013/03/27/from-socialization-to-social-change/
- "Clubwomen, The Pollitzer Sisters & The Vote." https://www.knowitall.org/series/sisterhood-sc-suffragists/clubwomen-pollitzer-sisters-vote
- Davis, Kimberlei N. "Orangeburg's glorious past: Two cemeteries resting places for notable pioneers." *The Times an Democrat,* November 3, 2013. https://thetandd.com/lifestyles/orangeburg-s-glorious-past-two-cemeteries-resting-places-for-notable-pioneers/article_6293f326-433b-11e3-879d-0019bb2963f4.html#tncms-source=login
- "Fiftieth Anniversary. South Carolina Federation of Colored Women's Club. 1909-1959." https://lcdl.library.cofc.edu/lcdl/catalog/lcdl:90342
- "The Great Branch Rosenwald Teacherage." https://www.greatbranchrosenwaldteacherage.com/
- Hine, William C. *South Carolina State University: A Black Land-Grant College in Jim Crow America.* Columbia, SC, The University of South Carolina Press, 2018, pp. 106-107.
- "History – South Carolina Federation of Women's Youth Clubs, Inc." https://www.scfwyc.com/history

- Jewell, Lucile. "The Marion Birnie Wilkinson Home." *The Southern Frontier*, vol. 1, no. 4, April 1940.

  The Southern Frontier, vol. 1, no. 4 [South Carolina Issue] · Social Welfare History Image Portal (vcu.edu)

- Jones, Cherisse R. "Wilkinson, Marion Birnie, June 23, 1870 – September 19, 1956." South Carolina Encyclopedia.

  https://www.scencyclopedia.org/sce/entries/wilkinson-marion-birnie/

- Jones, Devry Becker. "St. Paul's Episcopal Church." The Historical Marker Database,

- May 25, 2023.   https://www.hmdb.org/m.asp?m=223750

- Juanda Owens B. "Marion Raven "Mother Birnie" Birnie Wilkinson." Find a Grave, January 1, 2010.

  https://www.findagrave.com/memorial/46215038/marion-raven-wilkinson

- Lee, Maureen Elgersman. *Biographical Sketch of Marion B. Wilkinson.* Alexandria, VA, Alexander Street, 2016, p. 1.

- "Marion B. Wilkinson." September 2, 2023.

  https://en.wikipedia.org/wiki/Marion_B._Wilkinson

- "Marion Birnie Wilkinson." studySC.

  https://studysc.org/index.php/sc-people/marion-birnie-wilkinson

- "Marion Raven (Birnie) Wilkinson (1870 – 1956)," 2023.

  https://www.wikitree.com/wiki/Birnie-354

- "Dr. Robert S. Wilkinson, cira 1920." South Carolina State University (SC State). Celebrating the Collections of Historically Black Colleges and Universities.

  https://hbcudigitallibrary.auctr.edu/digital/collection/schc/id/2/

- "South Carolina Federation of Colored Women's Clubs." Wikipedia, December 19, 2021.

  https://en.wikipedia.org/wiki/South_Carolina_Federation_of_Colored_Women%27s_Clubs

- South Carolina State University. *Bulldog Yearbook,* 1957. South Carolina State University Historical Collection. p. 7.

- South Carolina State University Historical Collection.   First Lady Scholarship Luncheon program, "*Embracing Our Legacy and Building Our Future Through Excellence.*" February 27, 2004, p. 4.

President and First Lady Turner
Bulldog Yearbook, 1953

FIRST LADY
JULIA ELIZABETH ALLEN TURNER

**The Colored Normal, Industrial,
Agricultural and Mechanical College, 1950 - 1967**

Mrs. Julia Elizabeth Allen Turner served as the First Lady of South Carolina State College from 1950 – 1967. Mrs. Turner was married to Dr. Benner C. Turner, the Fourth President. They had two children, Elizabeth Ann Turner Klimas and Benner C. Turner, II.

After leaving S. C. State, Mrs. Turner retired with her husband to Somersworth, New Hampshire in 1968.

On August 11, 2008, Mrs. Turner's daughter, Mrs. Klimas, was interviewed by Mr. Travis D. Boyce. At the time, she was living in the United Kingdom as a retired educator and grandmother.

On September 8, 2008, Mrs. Turner's son, Benner, was interviewed by Mr. Boyce. At the time, he was an attorney in Venezuela and resided in Caracas. Mr. Turner graduated from Phillips Academy, Harvard University and Harvard Law School.

President Turner died on January 29, 1988 at Wentworth-Douglass Hospital in Dover, New Hampshire.

Family Photo *L-R: Elizabeth, daughter; Mrs. Turner; Benner, Jr., son. Bulldog Yearbook, 1961*

Staff of the Office of the President *Mrs. Evelyn D. Harris, Secretary; Mrs. Mary Moorer, Secretary; and Mrs. Julia A. Turner, Receptionist. Bulldog Yearbook, 1963*

BIBLIOGRAPHY

- Boyce, Travis D. *I Am Leaving And Not Looking Back: The Life of Benner C. Turner.* A Ph.D. dissertation, College of Education, Ohio University, June 2009, pp. 121-122.

- Reid, Richard. "S.C.state's fourth president: Dr. Benner C. Turner," June 11, 2008. https://thetandd.com/news/s-c-state-s-fourth-president-dr-benner-c-turner/article_17ea5764-a15e-5630-9440-6733ffd465bd.html

- South Carolina State University. *Bulldog Yearbook 1961.* South Carolina State University Historical Collection, p. 30.

- South Carolina State University. *Bulldog Yearbook, 1963.* South Carolina State University Historical Collection, p. 53,78.

- South Carolina State University Historical Collection. First Lady Scholarship Luncheon program. *"Embracing Our Legacy and Building Our Future Through Excellence."* February 27, 2004, pp. 4-5.

FIRST LADY
JULIE ETTA WASHINGTON NANCE

South Carolina State College, 1968 - 1986

Mrs. Julie Etta Washington Nance was an Orangeburg native who was born on the campus of South Carolina State College (SCSC) to the late J. Irwin and Julia R. Washington. The present Washington Dining Hall is named for her father. She attended Felton Laboratory School on the campus, graduated from Wilkinson High School in Orangeburg, South Carolina, and received the Bachelor of Science degree in elementary education from South Carolina State College in 1947.

In 1950, Julie married M. Maceo Nance, Jr., and they lived with her parents until they could build a residence next door. She taught first grade in Florence, South Carolina for one year, then returned to Orangeburg and worked in the college bookstore. Mrs. Nance became a stay-at-home mother after her two sons were born: Irwin Maceo Nance and Robert M. Nance.

Julie Nance devoted her entire life to SCSC and the Orangeburg community. Although she performed many duties with each, she was most noted for, and most proud of, her role as First Lady of SCSC where she served from 1967 to 1986. Her quiet charm, elegance and fondness for young people were reflected throughout her tenure as First Lady. During her nineteen-year tenure, she made the President's residence a home for all. Mrs. Nance was a gentle First Lady who nurtured students, provided leadership to faculty and staff, and served the community with both dignity and honor.

In *The Times and Democrat* December 2012 article, that reported on the death of First Lady Nance, it stated, in 1967, Benner C. Turner left as president and Maceo M. Nance, Jr. was named interim president. Just a few months later, on February 8, 1968, came the tragedy that has become known as the Orangeburg Massacre. In a 1995 interview, Mrs. Nance emotionally recounted being on campus and hearing the gunshots that took the lives of three young men and wounded about two dozen other students. She said the Nance family worked together to heal the emotional wounds of the college family and "unite the campus."

"First Lady Nance and her husband, who soon saw the word "interim" dropped from his title, went out of their way to mix and mingle with students, faculty and staff members, partly by having an open-door policy at their home and at the president's office."

"With his lifelong "soul mate" at his side, President Nance went on to become a builder not only of consensus but of brick and mortar as the college embarked on 35 construction and building projects, including the Smith-Hammond-Middleton facility, the Martin Luther King Jr. Auditorium, the I.P. Stanback Museum and Planetarium, a new student center, a new administration center, and new residence halls. Particularly close to his heart and a testimonial to his ability to overcome town-gown tensions was the Hillcrest Golf Course and recreational facility."

First Lady Nance received numerous awards, to include winning the Sammy Davis, Jr. Life Membership Achievement Award in 1985 and was awarded membership in the Club 100 Member of the NAACP for having written more than 100 NAACP memberships in one year. In 2001, she was the recipient of the Distinguished Alumna Award from South Carolina State University. Mrs. Nance held life membership in the NAACP and the SCSU National Alumni Association. She was also a member of Williams Chapel A.M.E. Church, Orangeburg, the Orangeburg Alumnae Chapter, Delta Sigma Theta Sorority, Incorporated, The Links, Incorporated, and an Emeritus member of The Regional Medical Center Foundation Board.

Special Edition | **Dr. M. Maceo Nance Jr., '49**
Fifth President of SCSU with wife Julie, '47

Photo: *Focus Newsletter, May 2001*

Hawaiian Luau given for the 1975 graduates. Bulldog Yearbook, 1976

Mrs. Nance says, *"I have had the opportunity to meet hundreds and hundreds and hundreds of young people and have maintained friendships with many of them. My family and I have had happy times and sad times ~ ~ we have enjoyed the life that we have had ~ ~ William Allen White says it best" ~" I am not afraid of tomorrow for I have seen yesterday and I love today."*

The Times and Democrat December 2012 article further expressed the community's attitude toward the work of the Nances. "The governor, five former governors, and 1,500 other guests attended the party in March 1986 that marked Nance's retirement after thirty-seven (37) years at the university, a record nineteen (19) of them as president. The Nances remained close to the university for the rest of their lives."

Mrs. Nance departed this life on December 30, 2012 in Orangeburg. She was preceded in death by her husband, Dr. M. Maceo Nance, Jr.; sister, Beverly (Perry) Knight, and brother, J.I. (Gloria) Washington, III. Mrs. Nance had a relatively small family: sons, Irwin Maceo (Toni) Nance and Robert M. (Tasha) Nance; two granddaughters, Michelle (Quentin) Nelson and Kimberly (Marvin) Colley; three grandsons, Nicholas Nance, Milligan Nance, and Kevin (Cherie) Hunt; four great-grandchildren, Mya Nelson, Maci Nelson, Madison Hunt, and Halie Hunt; two nieces, Gloria (Charles) Warner and Julie Lewis; one nephew, Perry David Knight; devoted friend and caregiver; Mrs. Dorothy Hodges; extended family; Mary Jeffries, Deborah Blacknall, Gloria Pyles; and other relatives and friends. Since her passing, two additional great grandchildren were born: Michael and Toni Colley.

President Nance died in Orangeburg on March 23, 2001 at seventy-four (74) years old. He and Mrs. Nance are buried at Belleville Memorial Gardens in Orangeburg, South Carolina.

The President and His Family *Robert Milton, student Orangeburg-Wilkinson High School (Belleville Campus); Irwin Maceo, Staff of State Development Board, Columbia, SC; Dr. M. Maceo Nance, Jr., President, and Mrs. Nance, the former Julie Etta Washington. (Photographed by Cecil Williams, 1975) Bulldog Yearbook, 1978*

BIBLIOGRAPHY

- "Julie Etta Washington Nance, former first lady of S.C. State, dies." *The Times and Democrat,* Dec 31, 2012, Updated Feb 18, 2020.

  https://thetandd.com/news/local/obituaries/julie-etta-washington-nance-former-first-lady-of-s-c-state-dies/article_c4a1a8fc-5303-11e2-b7cf-0019bb2963f4.html

- "Mrs. Julie Etta Washington Nance – Orangeburg." *The Times and Democrat,* Jan 1, 2013, p. 3.

  https://thetandd.com/news/local/obituaries/mrs-julie-etta-washington-nance---orangeburg/article_6631b62e-53d3-11e2-99b8-0019bb2963f4.html

- "Dr. M. Maceo Nance, Jr., '49 Fifth President of SCSU with wife Julie, '47." Cover photo. *Focus Newsletter*, Special Edition, May 2001.

- South Carolina State University. *Bulldog Yearbook,* 1976. South Carolina State University Historical Collection. p. 38.

- South Carolina State University. *Bulldog Yearbook,* 1978. South Carolina State University Historical Collection. p. 10.

- South Carolina State University Historical Collection. First Lady Scholarship Luncheon program, *"Embracing Our Legacy and Building Our Future Through Excellence."* February 27, 2004, pp. 4-5.

Photo: *Bulldog Yearbook, 1987*

FIRST LADY
SADIE BURRIS SMITH

South Carolina State College, 1986 – 1992

Mrs. Sadie Burris Smith was born in Aiken, South Carolina to parents Homer A. Burris and Adele Johnson Burris. Her siblings are Booker T. Burris, Ray E. Burris, Johnnie W. Burris, Loretta Burris Gaskin, and Evetta Burris Barrett.

She completed her education in the public schools of Aiken County. After graduating from Schofield Normal Industrial High School in Aiken, she earned a Bachelor of Science degree in sociology from North Carolina State A&T University in 1956. Later, she obtained a Master of Library Science degree from the University of Pittsburgh in 1974. She also holds teacher-librarian credentials which she utilized to provide services in K-12 public schools and higher education institutions.

Throughout her stellar career as a teacher-librarian, Mrs. Smith demonstrated that she was both an educator and an information manager with an integrated understanding of both areas. She combined knowledge of resource management, information services, personnel management, and information access systems, including information technology systems. She made valuable contributions to the many committees on which she served.

From 1986 to 1991, Mrs. Smith served as the First Lady of South Carolina State College. During her tenure, she was a strong advocate for Felton Laboratory School and the college and was genuinely concerned about the well-being of all students at both levels. Mrs. Smith worked closely with her husband, Dr. Albert E. Smith, who was the Sixth President, on various projects aimed at benefiting the students and improving the quality of their lives. Additionally, she contributed significantly to the community by participating in the Children's Reading Program at the Orangeburg County Library.

In 1987, a luncheon was held in honor of Mrs. Sadie Burris Smith, the First Lady, during the Inauguration ceremony of Dr. Albert E. Smith, the Sixth President of South Carolina State College. The success of the luncheon led to the idea of extending the gathering to address women's issues for the female employees at South Carolina State College. The initiative resulted in the inauguration of the "First Lady's Luncheon" for women on campus and in the community.

Workshops were organized in the luncheons for the years 1988, 1989, and 19990, covering various topics such as parenting, healthcare, woman-to-woman relationships, financial management, building self-confidence, retirement, consumerism, wills, insurance and estate planning, financial planning, and budget preparation. All luncheons were held on campus in the Kirkland W. Green Student Center.

- **February 25, 1987:** *"First Lady's Luncheon Honoring Mrs. Sadie Burris Smith."* Expressions of Goodwill from representatives: Board of Trustees, Mrs. Doris E. Johnson; Former First Lady, Mrs. Julie W. Nance; School of Education, Dr. Doris Matthews

- **February 16, 1988:** *"Today's Woman- Building Your Power Styles,"* speaker, Dr. Joyce Payne, Director, Office for the Advancement of Public Black Colleges, Washington, DC

- **February 14, 1989:** *TCYB – "Taking Care of Your Business,"* speaker, Ms. Sheila Johnson, Chaney, Producer, "Cross Talk," S.C. Educational Television, Columbia, SC

- **March 15, 1990:** *"Visionary Women --- Flexibility in the '90s,"* speaker, Dr. Patricia McCloud Russell, Attorney, Atlanta, GA

- **March 12, 1991:** *"Full Esteem Ahead,"* speaker, Ms. Kaycee Hale, Executive Director, Resource and Research Center, Fashion Institute of Design and Merchandising, Los Angeles, CA

Begun in 1987 to honor First Lady Sadie Burris Smith (shown above, at right), First Lady's Day provided the college with an opportunity to focus on women's issues in the workplace, family, and society. Dr. N. Joyce Payne (above, at the podium) was director of the office for the Advancement of Public Black Colleges of the National Association of State Universities and Land-Grant Colleges in cooperation with the American Association of State Colleges and Universities, and was the guest speaker at the 1988 First Lady's Day program. Mrs. Smith (below, at podium) described First Lady's Day as an opportunity to "develop a sense of unity at the institution, to foster a positive sense of self-worth and self-esteem as individual women, to develop effective communication techniques that will improve family, social, and work relationships, and to develop coping skills that will aid in the effective management of home and career responsibilities."

February 16, 1988

- **April 12, 1991:** *"The First Lady's Third Annual Jazz Concert."* SC State College Department of Music

Mrs. Smith is a member of Delta Sigma Theta Sorority, Incorporated, and The Links, Incorporated.

Mrs. Sadie Burris Smith and Dr. Albert E. Smith were married in June 1956. They have three children: Albert Clayton Smith, Robyne Smith Wilkerson, and Angela Smith Luster; four (4) grandchildren, and ten (7) great-grandchildren.

She currently lives in Charlotte, North Carolina. After fifty-seven (57) years of marriage, President Smith passed on November 17, 2013 in Pembroke Pines, Florida at eighty-one (81) years old.

Photo: *Christmas at the President's Residence Bulldog Yearbook, 1989*

BIBLIOGRAPHY

- Beatty, Robert. "Former FMU President Dies." *South Florida Times*. November 24, 2013.

  https://www.sfltimes.com/uncategorized/former-fmu-president-dies

- Smith, Albert Clayton. Interview. Conducted by Abbiegail Hamilton Hugine, December 2023.

- Smith, Sadie, Burris. Interview. Conducted by Abbiegail Hamilton Hugine, February 6-7, 2023.

- South Carolina State University. *Bulldog Yearbook,* 1987. South Carolina State University Historical Collection. p. 11.

- South Carolina State University. *Bulldog Yearbook,* 1989. South Carolina State University Historical Collection. p. 198.

- South Carolina State University Historical Collection. First Lady Scholarship Luncheon program, *"Embracing Our Legacy and Building Our Future Through Excellence."* February 27, 2004, pp. 5-6.

- South Carolina State University Historical Collection. First Lady's Day Luncheon program, *First Lady's Luncheon Honoring Mrs. Sadie Burris Smith,"* March 25, 1987.

- South Carolina State University Historical Collection. First Lady's Day Luncheon program, *"Full Esteem Ahead,"* March 12, 1991.

- South Carolina State University Historical Collection. First Lady's Day Luncheon program, *"TCYB – Taking Care of Your Business,"* February 14, 1989.

- South Carolina State University Historical Collection. First Lady's Day Luncheon program, *Today's Woman- Building Your Power Styles,"* February 16, 1988.

- South Carolina State University Historical Collection. First Lady's Day Luncheon program, *"Visionary Women --- Flexibility in the '90s,"* March 15, 1990.

FIRST LADY
PARTHELIA DAVIS CARPENTER

South Carolina State University, 1992

Mrs. Parthelia Davis Carpenter was born in Sumter, South Carolina on February 17, 1949. She was one of nine children, the seventh sibling, born to Willie and Emma Davis. Her siblings include Geneva Thomas, Blondell Tillman, Juanita Brown (deceased), Beatrice Woods, Anna Davis (deceased), Brenda WestPoint, Raymaynard Davis (deceased), and Alethia Tate (deceased).

Parthelia was a graduate of Lincoln High School in Sumter. She earned a Bachelor of Science degree in office management/administration from South Carolina State University. She served as the First Lady of South Carolina State College from January 13 to September 1992. During her tenure as First Lady, the college was granted university status on February 26, 1992.

Parthelia was a highly engaged member of the Orangeburg community. She was actively involved in several organizations, including Alpha Kappa Mu Honor Society, Jack and Jill of America, Incorporated, United Presbyterian Women, and The Association for Continuing Education. Furthermore, she had previously served as a member of the President's Advisory Council at Columbia Theological Seminary and Presbyterian College.

She was an active member of St. Luke Presbyterian Church and participated in the Chancel Choir. Additionally, she worked as a secretary/recorder for the Nominating Committee. Mrs. Carpenter pursued a professional career as an administrative specialist/counselor in Sumter County School District Number

17 and Richland County School District One in Columbia, South Carolina. After having worked for twenty-four (24) years in various positions at South Carolina State University, she retired in January 2000.

Her social activities included membership in the Thirteen Hearts Bridge Club, participation in the "SMASH" Dance Group for senior citizens, and membership in the St. Luke Line Dancers. She enjoyed community and church activities and retirement.

Mrs. Carpenter was married to Dr. Carl A. Carpenter, former Vice President for Academic Affairs and Interim President of South Carolina State University. At the time of her death, she and Dr. Carpenter had been married for fifty-one (51) years. They have two children: Carla Carpenter (Brian) Adams and Dr. Carl A. (Sharesa) Carpenter, II. Both children are graduates of South Carolina State University and professional educators; grandsons Attorney Brandon Carl Adams and Attorney Brent Carlton Adams, and granddaughters Karrington Lillian Carpenter and Kennedi Lauren Carpenter.

Parthelia was a resident of Orangeburg and passed away on December 15, 2018. She was laid to rest in Belleville Memorial Gardens in Orangeburg, South Carolina.

BIBLIOGRAPHY

- Carpenter, Carl A. Interview. Conducted by Abbiegail Hamilton Hugine, June 2023.

- Carpenter, Carla C. Interview. Conducted by Abbiegail Hamilton Hugine, August 2023.

- Funeral Services For The Late Mrs. Parthelia Davis Carpenter "Crunch," program, December 20, 2018.

- South Carolina State University Historical Collection. First Lady Scholarship Luncheon program, *"Embracing Our Legacy and Building Our Future Through Excellence."* February 27, 2004, pp. 6-7.

First Lady's Luncheon

FIRST LADY
CHRISTINE MCGILL DAVIS

South Carolina State University, 1996 – 2002

Mrs. Christine McGill Davis was born in Kingstree, South Carolina in 1950. She was the youngest of ten children born to Andrew and Carrie McGill, Sr. Christine attended the public schools of Williamsburg County and graduated from St. Mark High School in 1968 as the class salutatorian. She also completed her reign as homecoming queen.

After graduation, Christine enrolled at South Carolina State College in August 1969. She was successful in earning both bachelor's and master's degrees in speech-language pathology and audiology. During her course of study at SC State, Christine met her best friend and future husband, Leroy Davis, Sr. They got married on August 6, 1973.

Despite being a working wife and mother, Christine managed to travel extensively with her husband in the United States and abroad.

Christine Davis served as the First Lady of South Carolina State

First Lady's Luncheon: *First Lady Davis and Dr. Clemmie E. Webber, faculty member*

University from 1995 to 2002. During her tenure, she supported her husband, Dr. Leroy Davis Sr., who was the eighth president of the university. Christine's efforts helped establish the high standards of excellence that are reflected in the university's Annual Scholarship Gala and the STATE Room located at the Columbia Metropolitan Airport. She also played a significant role in supporting and hosting international students, which was a key focus during her time as First Lady. Throughout her tenure, Christine's quiet charm, elegance, and love for young people shone through.

Mrs. Davis had a fulfilling career as a public-school speech-language pathologist before retiring in 2002. She worked with children of different ages.

She is an active member of Mt. Calvary Baptist Church in Orangeburg and participates in Sunday Church School, Usher Board, and other auxiliaries. Her family and friends call her Christine or Chris. She enjoys reading, listening to various types of music, sewing, cooking, and having long telephone conversations with loved ones.

Christine and her husband reside in Orangeburg. They are the proud parents of two adult children: Tonya Javette Davis, District Instructional Specialist for Allendale County School District, Allendale, South Carolina; and Leroy, Jr., Senior Vice President, Head of Grant Administration at Wells Fargo Foundation, and six grandchildren: Taryn is a student at North Carolina A&T State University; Lauryn is a sophomore at the High School for Health Professions, Orangeburg;

Camille is a sophomore; Jessica is a freshman at the High School for Health Professions; Cayla is an eighth grader, and Leroy, III, is a fifth grader.

BIBLIOGRAPHY

- Davis, Tonya J. Interview. Conducted by Abbiegail Hamilton Hugine, September 2023.

- South Carolina State University Historical Collection. First Lady Scholarship Luncheon program, *"Embracing Our Legacy and Building Our Future Through Excellence."* First Lady Scholarship Luncheon program, February 27, 2004, p. 7.

FIRST LADY
FRANCES DAVENPORT FINNEY

South Carolina State University, 2002 – 2003

Mrs. Frances Davenport Finney, who describes herself as a farmer's daughter, was born on a large family farm in Newberry, South Carolina on November 10, 1933, to Leo and Beulah Butler Davenport. Before walking to school each day, Frances had to first attend to the chickens, milk the cows, and chop row after row of stubborn cotton. All of this farm work fed the family year-round. The Davenport family lived three miles from the Rosenwald Elementary school attended by the three Davenport children. The school was modeled after the traditional country schools of the day where classes were situated in one room and the rooms heated by a woodburning, potbelly stove. One of her most vivid memories happened one extra cold morning on her walk to school. When she arrived, she could no longer feel her fingers. Her teacher moved her near the wood burning stove and slowly lowered her frozen fingers into a bucket of water until she could feel them again. Young Frances' favorite subject was math.

Both parents influenced her, but her mother had the greatest impact

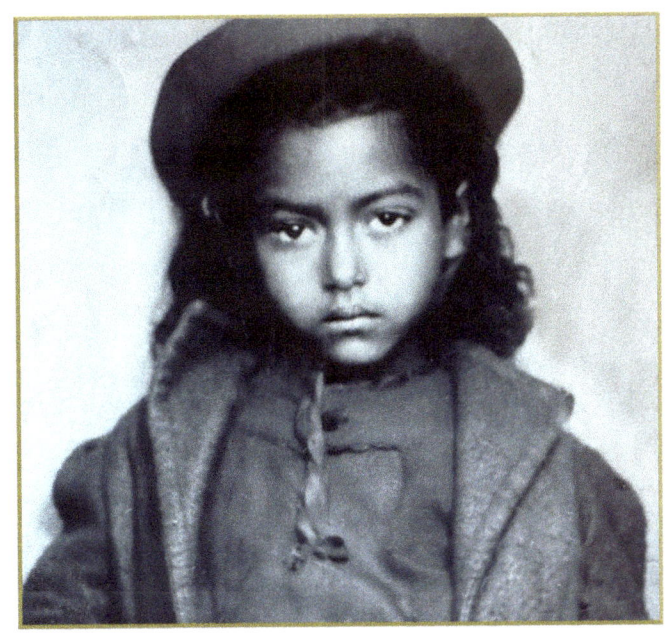

on her view of the world and on her values about life and living. Her family's closeness, strong work ethic, and unwavering belief in each generations responsibility to lift and climb was the deep root responsible for her success in life.

She worked hard in school and was not allowed to date until she was eighteen years old. At Drayton Street High School Frances Davenport dreamed of being a singer and actress just like one of her older cousins. But her family wanted her to forge a more responsible and dutiful life. She enrolled in Claflin College in 1951. At Claflin, Frances majored in early childhood education, pledged Alpha Kappa Alpha Sorority, Incorporated, and met the love of her life, a young South Carolina State law student, Ernest A. Finney, Jr., who also happened to be the son of the Dean of the College at Claflin. They married in August of 1955.

While raising her young family, Frances Davenport Finney kept her eye on every opportunity for more learning and excellence. She received her Master's Degree in education from South Carolina State College and continued with post-graduate study at Tuskegee Institute, North Carolina A& T University, and the University of South Carolina in Columbia.

Frances Davenport Finney spent her life dedicated to education, young people, and community outreach. She began her career teaching first grade in Bucksport, South Carolina. She went on to be Director of Kindergarten at Morris College in Sumter. She also taught non-traditional students in the Project T-Square program at the Vocational Rehabilitation Center in Sumter and ended her teaching career creating the Role Model to Success program as Director of Student Employment at the University of South Carolina-Sumter. This was a highly innovative and successful program geared toward high school students who were unsure of what to do with their lives and how to enter the workforce.

Mrs. Frances Finney, also known as "Ladybug," became First Lady of South Carolina State College (SCSC), when her husband, retired Chief Justice of the South Carolina Supreme Court, the first African American to be Chief Justice since Reconstruction, served as Interim President from July 1, 2002 until June 30, 2003. During her short tenure, she organized and promoted the Bulldog Round-Up Committee and directed various beautification endeavors across the campus. After securing business and community support, she led the charge for a grand gazebo to be built in the center of the campus. This was an exciting addition to the SCSC campus. In addition, a $500 student scholarship was established in honor of Frances D. "Ladybug" Finney and her indelible mark on historic South Carolina State University.

Mrs. Finney is legendary for the volunteer work she has done throughout her lifetime -- assisting in numerous community agencies, causes and events. On November 2022, Mrs. Finney celebrated her 89th birthday with family and friends. The highlight of the celebration was receiving a President's Lifetime Achievement Award from President Joe R. Biden. Mrs. Frances Davenport Finney was also presented with the highest Civil Award given in the United States to recognize her volunteerism.

After sixty-one years of marital bliss, Interim President Finney passed on December 3, 2017 in Columbia at eighty-six years old. He is survived by their children: Ernest Adolphus "Chip" Finney III, who maintains the family law practice in Sumter, South Carolina; their daughter, Nikky Finney, a poet and professor at the University of South Carolina-Columbia, and Jerry Leo Finney, Sr., an attorney with the Finney Law firm in Columbia, South Carolina; and five grandchildren.

Mrs. Finney currently lives in Columbia, South Carolina with her dog Alfie. She celebrated her ninetieth birthday in December 2023.

BIBLIOGRAPHY

- Brown, Moses. "Frances Davenport Finney honored by President Biden". *Carolina Panorama,* February 8, 2023. https://www.carolinapanorama.com/news/national/frances-davenport-finney-honored-by-president-biden/article_ceebc77a-a7ad-11ed-9878-2b68b853af9e.html
- Finney, Nikky. Interview. Conducted by Mary L. Smalls, January 23, 2024.
- *"First Black SC Chief Justice."* Photo. Cecil Williams South Carolina Civil Rights Museum.

- Logan, Sadye L. *In Their Own Voices*. Oral History Project & Documentary Interviews with Unsung Sheroes, *"Mrs. Frances Davenport Finney,"* The I. DeQuincey Newman Institute for Peace and Social Justice, 2007.

- South Carolina State University Historical Collection. First Lady Scholarship Luncheon program. *"Embracing Our Legacy And building Our Future Through Excellence,"* February 27, 2004, p.8.

FIRST LADY
ABBIEGAIL HAMILTON HUGINE

South Carolina State University, 2003 – 2007
Alabama A&M University, 2009 – 2021

Mrs. Abbiegail Mariam Hamilton Hugine was born in Green Pond, South Carolina, Colleton County. She is the eldest of eleven children born to Isiah and Viola Wright Hamilton. Her siblings, Brenda Hamilton Perkins, Theodore Hamilton (deceased), Isiah Hamilton, III, Theresa Hamilton, Deborah Hamilton Frazier, Timothy Hamilton, Eric Hamilton, Renee Hamilton Simpson, Audrey Hamilton Rushin, and Terrence Hamilton (deceased), grew up in a loving and nurturing family. Their parents were not high school graduates, but they were determined that all their children would go to college or be gainfully employed.

Abbiegail led the way by enrolling in Walterboro High School in Walterboro, South Carolina her last two years under the "Freedom of Choice" Federal Law. After graduating, she enrolled in South Carolina State College (University) in Orangeburg, South Carolina. In 1971, she graduated with a Bachelor of Arts degree in history; in 1975, a Master of Education degree in special education, and an ED.S. degree in education administration from the Citadel in Charleston, South Carolina.

Abbiegail taught at her alma mater, Walterboro High School, from 1971 to 1975 and worked in the Lansing Michigan School System from 1977 to 1978. Michigan State University awarded her a certificate in Teaching Emotionally Handicapped children.

Mrs. Hugine retired from Orangeburg Consolidated School District Five after a very successful career in education. At Orangeburg Consolidated School District Five, she was the director of The Technology Center, served as an instructional leader, and monitored and supervised all school operations. Her work at Orangeburg-Wilkinson (O-W) High School included assistant principal, administrative assistant, and chair of the Department of Social Studies.

Her professional development activities included working on the Orangeburg Consolidated School District Five Strategic Planning Committee; chair of the Social Studies Performance Goals; member of the SREB (Southern Regional Education Board), Making Schools Work Site Visit for Jasper County South Carolina public schools; and consultant with Stuart Flanagan in writing test items for the social studies Pact Test. Abbiegail was the administrative coordinator for O-W High School's Southern Association of Colleges and Schools Improvement Peer Review visit; the Freshman Academy administrator; High Schools that Work district coordinator; SACS Committee administrative chairperson; and presenter for numerous educational workshops on the local, regional, and national levels.

In recognition of outstanding work, services, and contributions, Abbiegail received several awards and honors including the Orangeburg School District Five Teacher of the Year; O-W High School Teacher of the Year; South Carolina Law Related Teacher of the Year; Soror of the Year for Beta Zeta Omega Chapter of Alpha Kappa Alpha Sorority, Incorporated; Mother of the Year for the Orangeburg Chapter of Jack and Jill of America; Outstanding Young Women of America; Clara Barton Award for service as chairperson of

The Hugine Family: Andrew III, Abbiegail, Akilah and President Andrew Hugine

the American Red Cross; Wil Lou Gray Outstanding Educator Award; and listed as Who's Who Among Outstanding Teachers.

In 2003, Mrs. Hugine became the First Lady of South Carolina State University (SCSU). Abbiegail was also instrumental in mentoring students to become stellar representatives of the University. She traveled extensively with her husband, President Andrew Hugine, Jr., as an ambassador to recruit students. During her tenure, she spearheaded four successful scholarship luncheons to raise funds for students.

***First Ladies**-L-R (seated): Julie Washington Nance, Frances Davenport Finney (back row) Christine McGill Davis, Parthelia Davis Carpenter, Abbiegail Hamilton Hugine, Sadie Burris Smith.*

- **February 27, 2004:** *"Honoring Former First Ladies of South Carolina State University,"* Kirkland W. Green Student Center

- **May 5, 2005:** *"Honoring the Former Miss SCSU Queens,"* Kirkland W. Green Student Center

- **May 12, 2006:** *"Honoring Distinguished Alumnae of SCSU,"* Kirkland W. Green Student Center

- **June 10, 2007:** *"Honoring Distinguished Women of Upstate South Carolina,"* Greenville, SC

After leaving SCSU in 2007, Mrs. Hugine served as First Lady at another HBCU, Alabama A&M University (AAMU) in Huntsville, Alabama, from 2009 to 2021. She hosted the inaugural First Ladies Scholarship Luncheon in 2011 followed by nine (9) more luncheons during her tenure. Before the 2021 luncheon, more than $250,000 had been raised to endow an AAMU scholarship for deserving students. Her work with The Normalite Walk Way Pavers Project generated more than $150,000 to provide scholarships to help students graduate from AAMU with degrees. Mrs. Hugine initiated an effort to enhance the beautification of the campus and continue the legacy of pride. Her work with the Bulldog Pride Committee and the precept of "Service is Sovereignty" was brought alive. More than $350,000 in scholarship funds were raised to help students graduate from college without huge loans.

Former South Carolina State University President Dr. Andrew Hugine, Jr. and his wife, Abbiegail, donated $50,000 to establish the Abbiegail and Andrew Hugine Endowed Scholarship for students at SC State. The contribution met the $100,000-lifetime giving threshold for their 2022 induction into the Thomas E. Miller Society which was established by Dr. Hugine during his presidency at SCSU. They are members of The Normalite Society established by President Hugine at AAMU. A $100,000 endowed scholarship at AAMU was established by Dr. and Mrs. Hugine. At each University, the Hugine name is visible on a building. The Andrew Hugine, Jr. Suites: A Living and Learning Community at SCSU honors Dr. Hugine, and the Andrew and Abbiegail Living and Learning Complex honors both at AAMU.

Abbiegail maintains membership at White Hall AME Church (former Jerusalem) where she was born and reared. She served as a trustee and a steward at St. John AME in Huntsville, Alabama, a member of the Huntsville Library Board for the Sparkman Library Project, a member of the Huntsville Botanical Gardens, and many more. She is a Golden member of Alpha Kappa Alpha Sorority, Incorporated, and an alumna of The Links, Incorporated. Her first book, *There Must Be Something in the Water: An Anthology of the Fourth Generation of Descendants of Green Pond after Emancipation*, is available at Amazon, Barnes and Noble, and other major outlets.

Dr. and Mrs. Hugine married in 1972 and have two children: Andrew Hugine, III, an educator, and Dr. Akliah Hugine Elmore, an engineer. They are blessed with family Karen Phillips Hugine, a social worker, and Quincy Elmore, a Senior Health Care administrator, and three beautiful grandchildren: Amir 10, Nylah 7, and Kal-el 3. Dr. and Mrs. Hugine reside in McDonough, Georgia.

BIBLIOGRAPHY

- South Carolina State University Historical Collection. *"Honoring Distinguished Alumnae of SCSU."* First Lady Scholarship Luncheon program, May 12, 2006.

- South Carolina State University Historical Collection. *Honoring Distinguished Women of Upstate South Carolina."* First Lady Scholarship Luncheon program, June 10, 2007.

- South Carolina State University Historical Collection. *"Honoring Former First Ladies of South Carolina State University."* First Lady Scholarship Luncheon program, February 27, 2004, pp. 4-8.

- South Carolina State University Historical Collection. *"Honoring the Former Miss SCSU Queens."* First Lady Scholarship Luncheon program, May 5, 2005.

- Clemons, Latoyia. "First lady's Scholarship Initiative Luncheon." *AAMU News*, March 14, 2017.

  https://www.wjab.org/aamu-news/2017-03-14/first-ladys-scholarship-initiative-luncheon

- "First Lady Scholarship Luncheon." *Speakin' Out News*, June 3, 2018.

  https://speakinoutweeklynews.net/2018/06/03/first-lady-scholarship-luncheon/

- "Mrs. Abbiegail Hugine 2019 First Lady's Scholarship Luncheon." *YouTube.* March 30, 2019.

  https://www.youtube.com/watch?v=uPvyeebNpnA

- "First Lady's Scholarship Event Cancelled." *AAMU News,* March 21, 2020.

  https://www.aamu.edu/about/inside-aamu/news/first-ladys-scholarship-brunch.html

- "First Lady's Scholarship Initiative Oct. 23." *AAMU News*, September 27, 2021. https://www.aamu.edu/about/inside-aamu/news/fsli-2022.html

- "Committee Members: About First Lady Abbiegail Hugine Founder and Committee Chair." *Bulldog Pride*. Alabama A&M University. https://www.aamu.edu/about/initiatives/bulldog-pride/committee-members.html

- "Bulldog Pride Committee Honored for Decade of Service." *AAMU News*. May 22, 2019. https://www.aamu.edu/about/inside-aamu/news/bulldog-pride-committee-honors-first-lady-hugine.html

- "Andrew And Abbiegail Hugine Living and Learning Complex." *AAMU News*. https://www.aamu.edu/campus-life/housing/residence-halls/hugine-complex.html

- "Hugines make $50,000 donation toward SC State scholarships." *The Times and Democrat*, January 20, 2022. https://thetandd.com/lifestyles/hugines-make-50-000-donation-toward-sc-state-scholarships/article_0dcaa000-bfe2-5e3f-9b57-0451a22a12c9.html

- "Hugines celebrate 50 years of marriage." *Walterboro Live,* February 3, 2023. https://walterborolive.com/stories/hugines-celebrate-50-years-of-marriage,60098

FIRST LADY
DIANE SHAW COOPER

South Carolina State University, 2008 – 2012

Mrs. Diane Shaw Cooper, the First Lady of South Carolina State University, was born to Reverend John Wesley and Mrs. Carrie Lee Shaw in Kingstree, South Carolina. Mrs. Cooper's amazing parents moved their large family to Eustis, Florida in 1954 where they grew up. Mrs. Cooper had six brothers and four sisters: Theotis L. Shaw, Christopher C. Shaw, John Wesley Shaw, III, Nollie S. Shaw, Jimmie C. Shaw, Matthew J. Shaw, Vertell S. Houston, Betty J. Shaw, Lucretia S. Collins, and Gwendolyn S. Benton.

Mrs. Cooper made history after graduating from Eustis High School, as she became the first African American student to enroll and graduate from the College of Human Sciences (formerly the School of Home Economics) at Florida State University in 1967 with a Bachelor of Science degree. She pursued further studies and obtained her Master of Education degree from Tuskegee University with a major in guidance counseling and student personnel services in 1975. Mrs. Cooper also completed her studies at the University of Illinois-Urbana and Trinity College of Washington, D.C.

On June 13, 2008, Mrs. Cooper retired from the Montgomery County Public Schools, Rockville, Maryland where she had enjoyed a successful and fulfilling career as a school counselor and resource counselor. Before that, she was a school counselor in the Huntsville, Alabama Public Schools, a Coordinator of Counseling for the ROTC Skills Center at Alabama A&M University, also in

Huntsville; supervisor of Counseling and Orientation at the Tuskegee University Job Corps Center, Tuskegee, Alabama; and a teacher of home economics in the Champaign County Public School, Champaign, Illinois and the Orange County Public Schools of Orlando, Florida.

Throughout her career, she received multiple awards and recognitions for her dedication and commitment. Some of these awards include Teacher of the Year, Educator of the Year, Apple Award, Eagle Award, Above and Beyond the Call of Duty Award, and Emerging Leader in the Alabama Association of Counseling and Development. She was also elected President of the Alabama Association for Counseling and Development, Chapter II.

Mrs. Cooper has received significant professional development by being a part of various organizations, including the National Education Association, Montgomery County Teachers Association, Potomac and Chesapeake Association of College Admissions Counselors, American Counseling Association, American School Counselors Association, Association for Multicultural Counseling and Development, and the Alabama Association for Counseling and Development.

Mrs. Cooper was an active member of her church, serving as a Bible study teacher, mission member and leader, deaconess, and member of the Baptist Women's Leadership Ministries Team for the DC Baptist Convention in Washington, DC.

On June 22, 1968, Diane Shaw married George Everett Cooper, her college sweetheart. They have two daughters, Nikki Angela and Carey Allison.

A March 26, 2009 interview by Dionne Gleaton for *The Times and Democrat* expressed many of Mrs. Cooper feelings. Upon arriving at South Carolina State University, as the new first lady, Mrs. Cooper said she was committed to student development and recruitment just like her husband, Dr. George E. Cooper, who will be inaugurated as S.C. State's 10th president on March 27th.

Diane Cooper said she took on her official role as the university's first lady with pride and saw it as an opportunity to be "the official hostess, ambassador and mother of the students there." "My love is students. My husband came in saying that he's student-centered without a doubt. I've been a high school counselor for numbers of years … I feel so honored now to have been almost transitioned to college. I've spent my entire profession … encouraging students to take advantage of higher education," Cooper said. "Now that I'm here, I feel that I'm pushing them on to greater things. She said her activities will center around enhancing her relationship with students and alumni."

Photo: *Dionne Gleaton T&D Staff Writer, March 26, 2009.*

Remarking about her beloved husband, she said, "I trust his judgment. He's intelligent; he's knowledgeable. I support him. I pray for him. I know that he's going to make wise decisions." My role is to embrace and support my husband's vision of being more student-centered," said Cooper, who has an extensive background of service to students.

She said her activities will center around enhancing her relationship with students and alumni. For example, she said she and Dr. Cooper had visited at least sixteen (16) alumni chapters across the nation, including Orlando and Chicago, in what she calls a "road show" designed to become more acquainted with chapter members.

Diane's March 26, 2009 First Lady Scholarship Luncheon focused on recognizing unsung heroes in education, fine arts, politics, health care, and law enforcement. The theme, *"Embracing Excellence: Meeting Tomorrow's Challenges,"* saluted faculty, staff, students, and community leaders.

The First Lady Scholarship Luncheon on March 26, 2010, had Donna Brazille as the keynote speaker. Brazile is a famous author, political commentator, and syndicated columnist. The theme of the event was *"Empowering Women and Building Self-Worth."* The event recognized 15 unsung heroes, including faculty members, staff, students, and community leaders in business, engineering, speech pathology, and audiology.

Photo: *Mrs. Emily England Clyburn, Ms. Donna Brazile, and First Lady Cooper*

Dale Linder from *The Times and Democrat* reported on the Luncheon. First Lady Cooper said she "added her own special touch to the luncheon. She turned it into a two-day affair that includes a Meet and Greet session on March 26 at Buckridge Plantation in Neeses. The luncheon will take place on Saturday, March 27, at The Cinema."

First Lady Cooper participated in the Council of President s and Chancellors' Spouses/Partners Summer Planning meeting in 2010 at Louisiana State University in Baton Rouge and in 2011 at Utah State University in Logan.

Photo: *Special to The T&D*

Other accomplishments during her tenure as First Lady included mentoring in the First Ladies Little Ladies Club at Felton Laboratory School. This program was designed to mentor and introduce the young ladies to the etiquette and recognition of academic success. A luncheon was held to formally induct the young ladies into the group. Ms. Mary Ravenell served as the advisor.

On August 15, 2023, Mrs. Cooper was recognized by Florida State University (FSU) for being among the first Black student enrolled at FSU between 1962-1971.

Mrs. Cooper currently resides in Florida. Her husband, President George E. Cooper, passed on Sunday, July 18, 2015 in Maryland. They were married for forty-seven (47) years.

BIBLIOGRAPHY

- Brown, Martha Rose. "Donna Brazile: 'This is our moment'." *The Times and Democrat,* March 28, 2010. https://thetandd.com/news/donna-brazile-this-is-our-moment/article_b6ae1f79-d8a2-5203-a515ddc268d90d75.html

- Cooper, Diane Shaw. Interview. Conducted by Abbiegail Hamilton Hugine, May and October 2023.

- Gleaton, Dionne. "S.C. State leader's wife sets her sights on student service." *The Times and Democrat,* March 26, 2009. https://thetandd.com/news/s-c-state-leaders-wife-sets-her-sights-on-student-service/article_c3e8b6f2-ed21-51bf-b73e-c89753da50a2.html

- Linder-Altman, Dale. "First lady hopes Brazile will help set record luncheon fund-raiser." *The Times and Democrat*, March 21, 2010. https://thetandd.com/news/first-lady-hopes-brazile-will-set-record-luncheon-fund-raiser/article_b48d488b-6010-5137-8925-cc19e3640d26.html-fund

- South Carolina State University. "Donna Brazile to Keynote SC State University's First Lady Scholarship Luncheon," A New STATE of Mind, E-Newsletter, March 11, 2010. https://www2.scsu.edu/files/E-Newsletter031110.pdf

- South Carolina State University Historical Collection, First Lady Scholarship Luncheon program, *Empowering Woman and Building Self-Worth,* March 26, 2010.

- South Carolina State University Historical Collection, First Lady Scholarship Luncheon program, *Recognizing Our Unsung Heroes,* March 26, 2009. https://www2.scsu.edu/files/2009FirstLadyLuncheonProgram.pdf

- "Twenty students inducted into Felton's Little Ladies Club." *The Times and Democrat,* April 23, 2011. https://thetandd.com/news/local/twenty-students-inducted-into-feltons-little-ladies-club/article_509b6be2-6c9f-11e0-865d-001cc4c03286.html

FIRST LADY
MONEDIA K. ELZEY

South Carolina State University, 2013 – 2015

South Carolina State University First Lady Monedia K. Elzey served along with her husband, President Thomas J. Elzey, the Eleventh President, to elevate the local, national, and global profile of the institution. They arrived at SC State in the summer of 2013.

A native of Woodstock, Virginia, Dr. Elzey received her Ph.D. and a post-master's certificate in Couple and Family Therapy from Drexel University, a Master of Social Work degree from Howard University, and a Bachelor of Social Work degree from Radford University.

For more than seventeen years, she was a psychotherapist in both community agencies and private practice. She has held various positions in management including program manager for a home health care agency and program director for a court-appointed foster care advocacy program.

Dr. Elzey was committed to advocacy and volunteerism. Her doctoral dissertation sought to improve services to victims of intimate partner violence by focusing on the screening practices of Couple and Family Therapists. She served on several not-for-profit boards including Women Organized Against Rape and the San Francisco Court Appointed Special Advocacy Program. She has held leadership positions in The Fairfax County Alumnae Chapter of Delta Sigma Theta Sorority, Incorporated and served as President of The Citadel Women's Club.

First Lady Elzey was actively involved in campus and student life by creating initiatives to ensure that each SC State student had an educational experience that prepared them for real-world challenges in a global society. One example was the First Lady's Boutique, a special place where students were provided, at no charge, with the tools to conduct a successful job interview complete with attire. As part of this initiative, she also hosted dinners at the Orangeburg Country Club where students could learn proper dining etiquette and how to professionally conduct themselves while dining in a business environment.

Dr. Monedia Elzey is pictured inside the First Lady Boutique, a place that provides professional attire and accessories, free of charge, to students for job interviews and business-related events. Larry Hardy/T&D

The First Lady's Scholarship Luncheon was held on February 28, 2014, in the Kirkland W. Green Student Center. The theme, *"Recognizing Legacy and Leadership,"* was addressed by the keynote speaker, the former Democratic presidential candidate Carol Moseley-Braun, and the first and only African-American woman elected to the United States Senate from Illinois. The Luncheon raised money for deserving and qualified students who otherwise would not be able to afford to attend college.

Dr. Elzey and her husband have two adult daughters, Tommi and Briana, and a two-year-old grandson, Mateo.

By Kimberlei Davis *The Times and Democrat*

BIBLIOGRAPHY

- Davis, Kimberlei. "Former senator says 'baton of freedom must not be allowed to fall on our watch'." *The Times and Democrat,* March 1, 2014. https://thetandd.com/news/former-senator-says-baton-of-freedom-must-not-be-allowed-to-fall-on-our-watch/article_c2fcaaa6-a0f5-11e3-82b2-0019bb2963f4.html

- Elzey, Monedia K. Interview. Conducted by Abbiegail Hamilton Hugine, February 8, 2024.

- "First Lady hosts Ambassador and former U.S. Senator Carol Moseley Braun." *The Times and Democrat,* February 28, 2014. https://thetandd.com/videos/first-lady-hosts-ambassador-and-former-u-s-senator-carol-moseley-braun/youtube_28fb6d24-a0e2-11e3-9eee-0019bb2963f4.html

- "First Lady's Scholarship Luncheon raises about $7K." *The Times and Democrat,* March 5, 2014. https://thetandd.com/news/first-lady-s-scholarship-luncheon-raises-about-7k/article_50800f8e-a3f9-11e3-9245-0019bb2963f4.html

- Hardy, Larry. "Dr. Monedia Elzey, first lady of South Carolina State University." *The Times and Democrat,* February 26, 2014, https://thetandd.com/dr-monedia-elzey-first-lady-of-south-carolina-state-university/image_3f6103f2-9f62-11e3-97ec-001a4bcf887a.html

- Hardy, Larry. "S.C. State University first lady reaches out through fundraising, boutique." *The Times and Democrat,* February 26, 2014, https://thetandd.com/article_36522b5c-9f61-11e3-94f1-001a4bcf887a.html.

- South Carolina State University Historical Collection, First Lady's Scholarship Luncheon program, *"Recognizing Legacy and Leadership,"* South Carolina State University. February 28, 2014.

FIRST LADY
AGATHA YOUMANS CONYERS

South Carolina State University, 2021 –

Agatha Youmans Conyers was born in Hampton, South Carolina to Jimmie E. Youmans and Gennett Robinson Youmans. She attended Ben Hazel K-2 School, Hampton Elementary 3-8 School, and Wade Hampton High School. After finishing high school, Agatha pursued higher education at South Carolina State College and graduated with a Bachelor of Science degree in Mechanical Engineering in 1986. In addition to her engineering degree, Agatha also earned degrees in interior decorating from Midlands Technical College in Columbia, South Carolina, a Master of Science degree in human service counseling from Liberty University in Lynchburg, Virginia, and a fundraising and philanthropy Certificate from Boston University.

Agatha has had a wide range of employment including Westinghouse-Hampton, South Carolina; Gates Rubber- Company, Moncks Corner, South Carolina; Freightliner Custom Chassis, Gaffney, South Carolina; United States Patent & Trademark Office, Alexandria, Virginia; Substitute Teacher on many Army Posts; United States Navy, Guantanamo Bay, Cuba; and The Bay Interior Design Furniture, Toronto, Canada.

As a military spouse, Mrs. Conyers has lived in seven states, South Korea, Cuba, and Canada. She is an avid volunteer, served as a school board member at Ft. Knox, Kentucky, led many organizations serving soldiers and their families, and served as a Girl Scout troop leader and a flag football coach.

Throughout her many moves, Agatha always found a church home and became very active wherever she called home. She has been a member of the Missionary Society, a Vacation Bible School leader and teacher, and a youth ministry leader. She is also a Dimond Life Member of Delta Sigma Theta Sorority, Incorporated, and was inducted into the Alpha Xi Chapter at SCSU in 1983.

Agatha assumed her role as the First Lady on September 30, 2022, at her alma mater. Since then, she has introduced various programs to assist students on campus. On September 29, 2022, the First Lady's Scholarship Luncheon was held at the Orangeburg County Conference Center to raise funds for scholarships. The event featured Charleston, South Carolina TV personality Octavia Mitchell as the keynote speaker. According to *The Times and Democrat,* First Lady Conyers stated during the event, "The scholarship will benefit all students, regardless of where they are in their educational journey. It is intended to help them stay in school." She added, "We are currently working on building the funds, and more information will be available soon. We aim to maintain the scholarship even after my tenure." Furthermore, Mrs. Conyers is interested in establishing a student chapel on campus to serve as a place of worship for students at SC State.

Additionally, *The Times and Democrat* reported speaker Linda Prince Johnson, First Lady Conyers' first cousin, as saying, "It is not by chance that she is here today in this place of honour. She is equipped with everything she needs to assist the President in taking this University to the next level." "The Youmans-Conyers Bulldog Legacy runs deep. Mrs. Conyers's grandparents are responsible for 17 graduates from SC state and six Bulldog marriages."

"The luncheon aimed to promote women's empowerment and emphasized the importance of health and wellness, particularly self-care. The program encouraged attendees to prioritize their health and well-being and regularly use positive affirmations starting with "I am." The event was part of a week-long celebration in honor of Mrs. Conyers's husband, Colonel (Retired) Alexander Conyers, who is the Thirteenth President of the university.

First Lady Conyers other initiatives include:

1. The SCSU Legacy Program that recognized incoming freshmen whose parents or grandparents attended the university

2. The Intellectual Properties for Social Change series which will provide students with insights on what a patent is and the process of protecting the rights to their ideas. The BECT (Business, Environment, Communications and Transportation) Institute sponsored the Intellectual Properties for Social Change series.

First Lady Conyers speaking at the launch of the Intellectual Properties for Social Change series. November 3, 2022. Facebook, SC State University.

On August 25, 2021, President Conyers and First Lady Conyers embarked on a $1.25 million campaign to commemorate the 125th anniversary of SCSU. In honor of their 40th anniversary, Delta Sigma Theta Sorority, Incorporated, Alpha Xi Chapter, donated $83,000 to SCSU as a tribute to their Line Sister First Lady Conyers.

She enjoys playing tennis, engaging in interior design, and fundraising. She actively participates in her church, serving as a Women's Church Ministry member and a Sunday School teacher. Due to her exceptional service, she has been awarded the Order of the Vivandiers, which is the highest Military Police Regimental Award given to spouses.

The Conyers Family L-R: Ace, Aly, Agatha, Alex

Agatha Youmans married Alexander Conyers on April 17, 1999. They have two children, Alexander, a 2023 graduate of SC State University, and Alyssa, a junior at The University of California Los Angeles (UCLA).

South Carolina State University First Lady Agatha Conyers (kneeling in yellow shirt) joins students in kicking off the inaugural Run the Yard Twilight 3K at the Chestnut Street pedestrian bridge on Tuesday evening, April 11, 2023. The event was part of the First Lady's campaign for a healthy SC State community.

BIBLIOGRAPHY

- Conyers, Agatha Youmans. Interview. Conducted by Abbiegail Hamilton Hugine, December 2023.

- First Lady's Scholarship Luncheon program, Orangeburg County Conference Center, September 29, 2022.

- SC State1896. "SC State University's First Lady's Scholarship Luncheon 2022." *YouTube.* https://www.youtube.com/watch?v=cdtl9jOGzrg

- SC State University. "SC State 1ˢᵗ Lady Agatha Conyers talks patents during Intellectual Properties for Social Change Series." *Facebook.* November 3, 2022. https://www.facebook.com/SCState1896/photos/a.476342645731863/6161227337243337/?type=3

- South Carolina State University. "Run the Yard Twilight 3K." https://scsu.edu/run-the-yard-twilight-3k

- *The Times and Democrat.* "SCSU's first lady to kick off intellectual properties series." October 31, 2022. https://thetandd.com/news/local/scsu-s-first-lady-to-kick-off-intellectual-properties-series/article_092e7f7c-33e0-5157-94e2-a8a740df74d9.html

- "'We are here to inspire generations to come.' SC State First Lady Agatha Conyers Luncheon held." *The Times and Democrat.* October 9, 2022. https://thetandd.com/news/we-are-here-to-inspire-generations-to-come-sc-state-first-lady-agatha-conyers-luncheon/articlec22f81af-6903-5fed-986e-0fcdf17be20c.html

AN OUTSIDE VIEW: REFLECTIONS

First Lady Julie Etta Washington Nance

- During my time in the Office of the President at SC State College, I had the pleasure of working with Mrs. Julie Nance, the esteemed First Lady. Her soft-spoken and endearing nature, coupled with her guidance on protocol, decorum, and social etiquette, proved to be invaluable to me throughout my tenure. It was evident that Mrs. Nance held herself to the highest standards of professionalism, as she was always seen wearing pearls or a necklace. I am grateful for the warmth and leadership she provided, and I still try to emulate the image she portrayed to this day.
  Debra Blackmon, '79
  Retired Executive Assistant, President's Office
  South Carolina State University

- Mrs. Nance lived a purposeful and meaningful life and demonstrating compassion and love for family, friends, South Carolina State College, and the community. She always presented herself in a professional, graceful, and elegant manner. Julie Nance was devoted to her role as first lady and the image that it represented. She supported, nurtured, motivated, and inspired students during good times and hard times. Mrs. Nance was one of a kind!
  Gloria D. Pyles, '70
  Title III Director
  SC State University

- Julie Etta Washington Nance, a quiet, gentle friend and First Lady of South Carolina State College epitomized exemplary service for students and the community. She served with dignity and honor. Her contributions were enumerable, especially to the NAACP. The president's home was one for all!

Margaret Anderson Roberts, '57

Retired Administrator, Orangeburg-Calhoun Technical College

Orangeburg, South Carolina

First Lady Sadie Burris Smith

"CHANCE MADE US NEIGHBORS, HEARTS MADE US FRIENDS!" This is an inscription on a small plate First Lady Sadie Burris Smith gave me as a departure gift when she and President Albert E. Smith moved back to Florida. This statement was true in 1993, and it rings even louder today!

We were neighbors and sorority sisters who cooked together, walked together, planned a wedding, attended luncheons, and interacted with the children of Faculty Row at South Carolina State College.

First Lady Smith and President Smith broke tradition when their residence adopted an "open door policy" for faculty, staff, students, and the children of Faculty Row. Every morning, the front door of the President's residence, located on the main thoroughfare of the campus, would be opened. From the outside, the inside foyer was visible to everyone who walked or drove past. First Lady Smith would greet the children and families with a warm handshake and an embrace, emanating her kindhearted persona. She was a very down-to-earth lady.

My children played games with her grandchildren in the den, and periodically ate their evening meal at "The President's Table." I remember the pan-smothered steak and onions I made in her kitchen as Dr. Smith watched.

When I raised the brown from the bottom of the pan, he exclaimed; "girl, you sure know what you're doing!"

Most mornings, Mrs. Smith and I walked our route from campus to Russell Street to Magnolia to Goff Avenue to Buckley and back to campus.

We planned her daughter Robin's wedding. Her adopted granddaughter, Whitney Lynne (my daughter), was the flower girl. She would marvel at Whitney's intellect and her ability, as a toddler, to spell "apple."

We were sorority sisters of the Orangeburg Alumnae Chapter of Delta Sigma Theta Sorority, Incorporated. We got together often to discuss sorority business after our monthly meetings.

After moving to Florida Memorial College, we remained friends. I attended their retirement ceremony (June 2006) and farewell breakfast the next day. I remember relaxing, sitting, and talking on the back porch of their beautiful home overlooking the golf course in Pembroke Pines, Florida. The memory from over thirty years ago still remains very vivid in my mind today!

She lost her college sweetheart, President Albert E. Smith in November of 2013. He was laid to rest on one of the coldest days I ever witnessed in Greensboro, North Carolina. After returning to North Carolina, I attended her family reunion and got to know the Burris family. I taught her niece, Natombi Smith, at South Carolina State University.

We have remained friends through the years. We spend late nights chatting on the phone and making unkept promises to visit each other. Our friendship has endured all tests of time and will continue to endure because "Chance made us neighbors, hearts made us friends!" *We are Best Friends for Life!! I love you!*

Mary Worley-Jordan '72
Retired Professor, Department of English
South Carolina State University

First Lady Abbiegail Hamilton Hugine

To me, Mrs. Abbiegale Hamilton Hugine is the woman described in Proverbs 31. She is a phenomenal woman; she does noble things; her beauty is fleeting, and her charm is unmatched.

I have known her for many years, and in my eyes, she has always been a First Lady. She has always been deeply concerned about others, especially the students at South Carolina State University. She always exemplified high standards and represented the University with dignity and grace. To me, she was and will always be a phenomenal First Lady.

Doris Johnson Felder, '76
Reference Librarian, Miller F. Whittaker Library
South Carolina State University

The First Ladies

Recent First Ladies of South Carolina State University

Of the nine women who served as first ladies of South Carolina State University between 1967 and 2024, some I knew better than others. While they were each unique individuals in background, temperament, and personality, they all exhibited similar traits in that they were friendly and conscientious representatives of the University who served as valuable assets to their husbands. Some seemed more comfortable than others in their public role on the campus and in the community. In my judgment and without naming names, at least one or two of them would have made more effective presidents of South Carolina State than their husbands.

Julie Nance: M. Maceo Nance. Jr. was named interim president in 1967. His wife Julie became the "interim" first lady. Both Maceo and Julie Nance were graduates of South Carolina State College. The 1967-68 school year was the most tragic and difficult year in the history of the institution. On February 8, 1968, three students were shot and killed and at least 28 others were injured when

South Carolina Highway patrolmen opened fire on the unarmed students in what came to be known as the Orangeburg Massacre. Only months after assuming leadership roles, the Nances had to comfort students and families whose lives had been torn apart by the tragedy. The Nances did so with compassion, understanding, and resolve. Two months after the Massacre, the campus was again plunged into sadness when Dr. Martin Luther King was assassinated. In June 1968, Maceo Nance was named president of South Carolina State, and Mrs. Nance was no longer the interim First Lady. Over the next 18 years until President Nance's retirement in 1986, Mrs. Nance was a constant and reassuring presence on the campus and at numerous community events.

Parthelia Carpenter: Carl Carpenter was a superb administrator and fine interim president. But I never had an opportunity to get acquainted with his wife. Other people who I knew were generous in their praise of Mrs. Carpenter.

Sadie Smith: The wife of President Albert E. Smith was a warm and engaging first lady. Easy to talk to, she seemed to relish her role representing the University. While I had a sometimes-bumpy relationship with President Smith after he and the Board of Trustees decided to award an honorary doctorate to U. S. Senator Strom Thurmond, I found Mrs. Smith to be affable and not much bothered by the political controversy. Moreover, President Smith and I worked to patch matters up. His wife remained a steady influence who—like her husband—carried no grudges.

Christine Davis: President Leroy Davis, Jr. and I got along well. He was a former student of mine, and he was a member of the same graduating class as Andrew and Abbiegail Hugine. Davis's wife Christine was a pleasant first lady with a ready smile who I regret that I never got to know very well.

Frances Finney: Known by many as "Ladybug," Mrs. Finney was an enthusiastic first lady. She eagerly embraced her role as first lady and worked hard to promote her husband and the University. She enjoyed the "spotlight" while

Judge Finney seemed more reluctant and reticent in his public appearances than his charming and gregarious wife.

Abbiegail Hugine: Abbiegail Hamilton and her future husband, Andrew, were both students—outstanding students—in U. S. history classes that I taught during my first year and their first years at South Carolina State in 1967-68. Mrs. Hugine became a teacher and administrator who was devoted to her students and their advancement. More than once, she invited me to speak to her classes about the Orangeburg Massacre. She has a passionate interest in education, in history and in South Carolina State University.

Diane Cooper: Mrs. Cooper was a wonderful first lady. Easy to engage and with no pretensions whatsoever, she readily agreed to serve on the Friends of Miller F. Whittaker, the group supporting and assisting the library. No mere figurehead, she took her role and responsibilities seriously as a working member of the Friends. She was as diligent as any member of the Friends' board.

Monedia Elzey: I do not recall having met or becoming acquainted with Mrs. Elzey.

Agatha Conyers: Mrs. Conyers and her husband, Col. Alexander Conyers, inherited a challenging and difficult situation when he became President of South Carolina State, and she became the first lady. She is at ease in public gatherings and demonstrates a genuine interest in the activities and concerns of others whether they are students, faculty members, or people in the community.

Dr. William C. Hine
Retired Professor Emeritus of History
South Carolina State University
26 January 2024

- Mrs. Julie Nance is widely regarded as one of the most exceptional first ladies in history. She was a kind and genuine person who set the bar high for others in her position. Julie was a perfect example of an altruist, and she served in her role with elegance, grace, and class for nearly twenty years. She embodied the bulldog spirit and was a strong supporter of faculty, staff, and students alike.

- Mrs. Sadie Smith was a caring and student-focused first lady who was highly concerned about student success. She was warm, elegant, gracious, and always greeted everyone with an endearing smile.

- Mrs. Diane Cooper was an exemplary first lady who was known for her kindness, gentleness, and compassion. She was one of the strongest advocates for the students and was equally committed to the welfare of the faculty and staff. During difficult times, she assisted them in meeting their needs. Diane was a truly wonderful and caring person who left a positive impact on everyone she encountered.

Mary E. Jeffries
Retired School Counselor
Dorchester County School District #4
St. George, South Carolina

- First Lady Nance worked to keep the college and the Orangeburg community communicating. I remember participating in events during the holidays and on other occasions at the President's home when the coaches' wives served as hostesses.

Mrs. Nance was a very active member of Williams Chapel AME Church in Orangeburg. She served on various committees and assisted in guiding the church in completing many of its goals.

- I have very fond memories of the first time First Lady Sadie Burris Smith visited our library. During our conversation about the different collections and holdings we had, I mentioned that we were in the process of organizing the Historical Collection (archives). She quickly offered to help and use her skills as a trained librarian. First Lady Smith came every Friday afternoon for three hours over two months until we hired an archivist. Her warm-hearted support of our library and university, as well as her graceful demeanor, left a lasting impression on me.

Minnie M. Johnson
Retired, Head of Reference, Miller F. Whittaker Library
South Carolina State University

- It was an honor and privilege to serve the elegant First Ladies of South Carolina State University. Each First Lady exemplified dignity, grace, kindness, and that Classy Bulldog tenacity. I will forever cherish each one of them. They treated me like family.

Lacella Williams
Retired Housekeeper, President's Residence
South Carolina State University

CREDITS

The success of this project is due to the contributions and input of many persons. Many thanks to each of them for their assistance in compiling this book on the *First Ladies of South Carolina State University*.

Miss B. A. Johnson, retired rducator, Huntsville, Alabama,
and author of three books, *Sassy Discovers the AME Church, Sassy Uncovers Peter Allen's Secret, and Pandemonium in Puzzle Town*, for the inspiration to write this book. She is also a dear friend and church sister of Abbiegail.

Authors

Mrs. Abbiegail H. Hugine	First Lady, South Carolina State and Alabama A&M Universities
Ms. Mary L. Smalls	Retired Dean, Library and Information Services, Miller F. Whittaker Library, (South Carolina State University)

Editorial Review

Dr. Andrew Hugine, Jr.	Retired President, South Carolina State University, President Emeritus, Alabama A&M University, and Spouse of Co-Author, First Lady Abbiegail H. Hugine

Contributors

Colonel (Retired) Alexander Conyers	Thirteenth President, South Carolina State University
Mrs. Agatha Youmans Conyers	First Lady, South Carolina State University
Mr. Irwin Maceo Nance	Son of First Lady Julie Etta Washington Nance and President Maceo Nance, Jr.
Mr. Robert M. Nance	Son of First Lady Julie Etta Washington Nance and President M. Maceo Nance, Jr.
Mrs. Sadie Burris Smith	First Lady, South Carolina State College
Mr. Albert Clayton Smith	Smith and President Albert E. Smith
Dr. Carl A. Carpenter	Interim President, South Carolina State University, Retired Administrator, and Spouse of First Lady Parthelia Davis Carpenter
Mrs. Carla C. Adams	Daughter of First Lady Parthelia Davis Carpenter and Interim President Dr. Carl A. Carpenter
Ms. Tonya J. Davis	Daughter of First Lady Christine McGill Davis and President Leroy Davis, Sr.
Mrs. Frances Davenport Finney	First Lady, South Carolina State University
Ms. Nikky Finney	Daughter of First Lady Frances Davenport Finney and Interim President Ernest A. Finney, Jr., Chief Justice South Carolina Supreme Court

Mrs. Diane Shaw Cooper	First Lady, South Carolina State University
Dr. Monedia K. Elzey	First Lady, South Carolina State University
Mrs. Shondra C. Abraham	Alumna, Chief of Staff, President's Office, South Carolina State University
Ms. Deborah Blackmon	Alumna, Retired Executive Assistant, Office of the President, South Carolina State University
Mrs. Barbara Randall Clark	Alumna, Retired Educator, Orangeburg School District 5, Author and Presenter
Mr. Avery L. Daniels	Alumnus, Archivist, South Carolina State University Historical Collection, Miller F. Whittaker Library
Dr. Sarah W. Favors	Retired Professor Emeritus, Department of English, South Carolina State University
Mrs. Doris Johnson Felder	Alumna, Reference Librarian, Miller F. Whittaker Library, South Carolina State University
Dr. William C. Hine	Retired Professor Emeritus of History, South Carolina State University and author of *South Carolina State University: A Black Land Grant College in Jim Crow America*
Mrs. Mary E. Jeffries	Retired School Counselor, Dorchester County School District #4, St. George, South Carolina

Mrs. Minnie M. Johnson	Retired, Head of Reference, Miller F. Whittaker Library, South Carolina State University
Mrs. Cathi Mack	Alumna, Assistant to the Dean, Coordinator of Technical Services, Miller F. Whittaker Library, South Carolina State University
Ms. Gloria D. Pyles	Alumna, Title III Director, South Carolina State University
Reverend Mary E. Ravenell	Alumna, Retired Educator, Felton Laboratory School, South Carolina State University
Mrs. Margaret Anderson Roberts	Alumna, Retired Administrator, Orangeburg-Calhoun Technical College, Orangeburg, South Carolina
Mr. Cecil J. Williams	Curator, Cecil Williams South Carolina Civil Rights Museum, Orangeburg, South Carolina
Mrs. Lacella Williams	Retired Housekeeper, President's Residence, South Carolina State University
Ms. Mary Worley-Jordan	Alumna, Retired Professor, South Carolina State University

SOUTH CAROLINA STATE UNIVERSITY PRESIDENT RESIDENCES

President's Residence
Bulldog Yearbook, 1961, p. 22

The stately residence, known to several generation as "the White House" was demolished to make way for the present dining hall. A landmark on the cmapus for many years, its passing from the scene was lamented by many alumni and members of the State College family.

President's Residence (1961) *Bulldog Yearbook, 1963, p.111*

Andrew Hugine, Jr. Suites: A Living & Learning Community *(Dedication: October 2007)*

About Abbiegail H. Hugine

Abbiegail earned bachelor's and master's Degrees from South Carolina State University and an Educational Specialist degree from The Citadel. She is a retired educator-administrator, having worked 37 years in Walterboro, South Carolina; Lansing, Michigan; and Orangeburg, South Carolina. She is the creator of *Spoils and Return*, a website designed as a virtual community for grandparents to share interesting stories, accomplishments, and past times of their grandchildren. As a retiree, her time is spent volunteering in her church and community.

She loves traveling, reading, and taking care of her grandchildren. She is the author of *There Must Be Something in the Water: Anthology of the Fourth Generation Descendants of Green Pond after the Emancipation*, a book chronicling the accomplishments of individuals from her small hometown of Green Pond, South Carolina. She holds membership in White Hall AME Church; St. John AME Church; Greater Huntsville Chapter of The Links, Incorporated; Alpha

Kappa Alpha Sorority , Inc.; and she recently served on the advisory council of Huntsville Madison County Botanical Gardens and Friends of North Huntsville Public Library.

Abbie was the First Lady at South Carolina State University (SCSU) and Alabama A&M University (AAMU). She is married to Dr. Andrew Hugine, Jr., former President of SCSU and President Emeritus of AAMU. They are the parents of two children, Andrew Hugine, III and his wife Karen; and Akilah Hugine-Elmore and her husband Quincy. She has three lovely grandchildren, Amir, Nylah, and Kal-el.

About Mary L. Smalls

Mary is a native of Salley, South Carolina, and was the 1965 salutatorian at A. L. Corbett High School in Wagener, South Carolina. In 1974, she graduated from South Carolina State College with a Bachelor of Science degree in education. She received her master's (1975) and specialist (1987) degrees in librarianship from the University of South Carolina-Columbia. Mary worked as a librarian at Voorhees College in Denmark, South Carolina, the secondary schools in Elloree and Orangeburg, and retired as dean of library and information services at the Miller F. Whittaker Library at South Carolina State University. She co-chaired two presidential inaugurations (Drs. Hugine and Davis); chaired and co-chaired the Founders' Day Committee, which included the First Lady's Scholarship Luncheon; and was one of the co-founders of the Friends of the Miller F. Whittaker Library.

She serves her community as a volunteer for the Meals on Wheel program, a board member of The Samaritan House of Orangeburg County homeless shelter, a board member of the Orangeburg County Library, and a member of the executive committee and life member of the Orangeburg Branch NAACP. She is also a life member of the South Carolina State University National Alumni Association.

Mary is passionate about reading and preserving history as it unfolds. She believes historical materials provide guidance, foster critical thinking, and connect the past, present, and future generations with enjoyment, appreciation, and exploration.

She has two sons, Eric and Eryl (Keisha) Smalls; one granddaughter, Lauren M. Smalls; a bonus grandson, Jonah L. Adams; two step-granddaughters, Serena and Ariana Davis; and a step- great-granddaughter, Nova Davis.

FRESH INK GROUP
Independent Multi-media Publisher
Fresh Ink Group / Push Pull Press
Voice of Indie / GeezWriter

Hardcovers
Softcovers
All Ebook Formats
Audiobooks
Podcasts
Worldwide Distribution

Indie Author Services
Book Development, Editing, Proofing
Graphic/Cover Design
Video/Trailer Production
Website Creation
Social Media Marketing
Writing Contests
Writers' Blogs

Authors
Editors
Artists
Experts
Professionals

FreshInkGroup.com
info@FreshInkGroup.com
Twitter: @FreshInkGroup
Facebook.com/FreshInkGroup
LinkedIn: Fresh Ink Group

There Must Be Something in the Water

Anthology of the Fourth Generation Descendants of Green Pond after the Emancipation

Abbiegail Mariam Hamilton Hugine

Scan to watch the Trailer on YouTube

Scan to order now from Amazon!

A small rural community in the Low Country along Ocean Highway, Green Pond, South Carolina, has long lacked cultural and educational opportunities for its young people's future success. Still, many have gone on to serve in the highest levels of education, government, public service, elected office, business, and medicine. So much success against the odds suggests surely There Must Be Something in the Water. Abbiegail Hugine chronicles the impact just 42 of Green Pond's many children have gone on to make in the world. These inspirational stories prove that, regardless of one's background, we can all find our own paths toward greatness.

Full-color Interior
8.5-inch Square
Laminate Hardcover
Full-sized Softcover
All Ebook formats

As We Remember
A History of the Woman's Relief Corps
In Beaufort, SC

Najmah Thomas
Fred Washington, Sr. Woman's Relief Corps No. 1 of SC

This book documents the remarkable story of a Woman's Relief Corps (WRC) chapter in Beaufort, South Carolina. The WRC is a national organization established as an official auxiliary to the Grand Army of the Republic (GAR) in 1883. A Woman's Relief Corps post has existed in the city of Beaufort, South Carolina, in various forms since 1892 when GAR Post David Hunter No. 9 was established in the city, with statesman Robert Smalls selected as Post Commander in 1894.

While much of the record of the early Beaufort WRC was passed on through the esteemed oral history tradition, in 2019 members commissioned a study with the purpose of ensuring their story would be documented in print form and told for many generations to come. That story intentionally centers African American women as lead agents of change and co-creators of the patriotic spirit, an important theme given the fact that historically the national WRC was primarily White-led, and in southern localities like Beaufort, completely segregated.

Beyond the Corps' main purpose of documenting their lived experiences as WRC members, this story is compelling in the larger context as the nation contends with changing notions of its national identity and definitions of patriotism.

Laminate Hardcover
Softcover
All Ebook Editions